Arkansas and the New South
1874–1929

Histories of Arkansas
Elliott West, general editor

ARKANSAS

the *New South*

1874–1929

CARL H. MONEYHON

The UNIVERSITY *of*
ARKANSAS PRESS
Fayetteville   1997

12 11 10 09 08   9 8 7 6 5

Designed by A. G. Carter

⊖ The paper used in this publication meets
the minimum requirements of the American
National Standard for Permanence of Paper
for Printed Library Materials   Z39.48-1984.

LIBRARY OF CONGRESS CATALOGING-
IN-PUBLICATION DATA
    Arkansas and the New South, 1874–1929 /
Carl H. Moneyhon.
        p.   cm. — (Histories of Arkansas)
    Includes bibliographical references (p.   )
and index.
    ISBN 1-55728-489-x (cloth : alk. paper). —
ISBN 1-55728-490-3 (paperback : alk. paper)
    1. Arkansas—History—1865–
I. Title. II. Series.
F411.M74   1997
976.7'05—dc21   97-26932
                                 CIP

*This project is supported in part by a grant
from the Arkansas Humanities Council and
the National Endowment for the Humanities.*

Contents

Illustrations

The following illustrations appear after page 60.

Families

Labor's Many Faces

Changing Surroundings

Foreword

Fewer books of history have been written on Arkansas than on any other state. We can speculate on the reasons. Perhaps Arkansans have felt themselves in the shadow of larger neighbors with legions of vigorous boosters. The state's remarkable diversity within a relatively small area may have frustrated the search for the grand unifying themes that historians love. Whatever the cause of this neglect, however, two things can be said with certainty. The lack of attention is unjustified, and all of us, especially Arkansans, have been the poorer for it.

The Histories of Arkansas Series is a step toward illuminating Arkansas history, both by telling the state's story and by encouraging others to pursue and write about its many byways. Each volume in the series comes from a specialist in state and regional history. Each will be written as an engaging story that all interested readers will find enjoyable. While the authors will help readers see the themes that help us understand the broadest meaning of our state's past, they will also take special pains to recreate the daily lives of ordinary Arkansans, from the earliest Native Americans more than ten millennia ago to the first European-American settlers, survivors of the grim years of the Civil War and its stormy aftermath, and the families who have seen the wrenching changes of this century.

It would be difficult to imagine a worthier book to inaugurate the series than Carl H. Moneyhon's *Arkansas and the New South*. For nearly a generation Moneyhon has been widely recognized as a leading historian of Arkansas and the American South during the late nineteenth and early twentieth centuries. A student of John Hope Franklin, a giant among African-American historians, Moneyhon has shown us the way to a much fuller appreciation of the experience of black Arkansas, especially during the years after the Civil War. In *Arkansas and the New South*, he brings his seasoned knowledge to bear on the crucial years between the end of Reconstruction and the start of the Great Depression.

The story he tells is fascinating—and not without its unexpected turns. There is a well established historical image of Arkansas during these years. While most of America and much of the South awakened to new possibilities, this image has it, Arkansas rolled over and continued to doze. The portrait painted by Moneyhon is not so simple. Like all Southern states, Arkansas faced enormous problems inherited from the devastation and turmoil of the Civil War. Difficulties were compounded by the need to reckon with extraordinary transformations in the nation at large as the United States emerged within a few generations as a modern industrial state, an urban society, an economic behemoth, and a world power. Moneyhon traces Arkansas's responses to these formidable challenges. The Arkansas he describes was stirring with economic changes and wrestling with political issues even more tortured than usual. Its towns and cities were surprisingly vibrant, troubled, and enriched by their peculiar variations of the profound changes unfolding throughout urban America. Moneyhon finds that race relations, while appalling enough, had surprising subtleties. Arkansas, in short, was experiencing far more vigorous change than the usual accounts would have it. In that light, the events at the end of Moneyhon's story, the calamitous onset of the Great Depression, take on an even greater significance.

Arkansas and the New South reminds us of what many Arkansans have known all along—that their state's history is still largely untold. Future volumes in the Histories of Arkansas Series will consider our long Native American heritage, exploration and the colonial era, the territorial years and early statehood, the trauma of the Civil War and the tumult of Reconstruction, and the transforming decades from the Great Depression until today. Moneyhon's fine contribution, set in the middle of this long and complex history, invites readers to explore the Arkansas past both before and after it. As *Arkansas and the New South* shows us, it is an exciting prospect.

Elliott West
University of Arkansas, Fayetteville

Introduction

History attempts not only to describe events of the past but to analyze them, to characterize and explain them. Years within which events and trends seem to fit together are linked together as historical eras. One of the most significant of these in Arkansas history, and that of the South as a whole, is the years associated with efforts at producing what was called the New South. Emerging from fifteen years of Civil War and Reconstruction, the state and region faced the difficult task of reintegrating themselves into a nation engaged in an economic and social revolution associated with the development of national markets, industrialization, and urbanization. At least for Arkansas, this process and its outcome have received little scholarly attention.

Despite the lack of an extensive historical literature and the fragmented nature of much that exists, there are plenty of assumptions made about the state's history during these years, particularly about the forces determining the extent to which Arkansas conformed itself with national economic and social trends. Without question, it is recognized that Arkansas failed to achieve the economic success many hoped for during this era, although the extent of that failure is debatable. The main questions have centered on how to explain the result.

In giving their whys, scholars have often embraced the interpretations developed by popular culture. Few, though, would probably agree with the harshness of H. L. Mencken's attack upon Arkansas when he called it "the most shiftless and backward State in the whole galaxy" and concluded that Arkansans were "too stupid to see what is the matter with them." Nonetheless, the idea that somehow Arkansas's cultural roots and its own people prevented the state's progress is a recurring concept in Arkansas scholarship.

In its more positive form, this cultural-determination thesis appears in the so-called Ozark Tradition Myth, which views the Ozarks and other mountain regions as part of an isolated community living a lifestyle unchanged until the 1940s. These self-reliant subsistent farming families led lives and possessed values that might appear desirable in the modern world, but they also had little use for change and served as a barrier to anything that might have pushed Arkansas forward economically.

A more negative view portrays the state as a society dominated by the culture of the Old South. Racism, brutality, and violence were the molding forces in the state's past. Brutal planters and landowners exploited labor, suppressed African Americans, and dominated Arkansas politics. Desiring as little change as possible, this group blocked the way of progress in the state.

In *Arkansas Odyssey*, Michael Dougan put both of these themes together. Dougan saw the course of Arkansas history as the result of a struggle between forces of tradition, clearly sustained by the landed classes of the Delta and the self-sufficient farmers of the hills, against those interests desiring change. With power and numbers sustaining the status quo, the possibilities of change were always limited.

In fact, the very premise about Arkansas's identity or the result of the state's reintegration effort (upon which much modern scholarship is built) has hardly been tested. What research and publication has been done suggests that the state may not have been as much of a failure as previously assumed. If so, then the various explanation of events seems hardly to work. This study takes a new look at Arkansas during the New South Era from 1874 to 1929, seeking to determine what happened overall to its economy and society when given the opportunity to reintegrate itself into the national mainstream. It also seeks to explain the forces at work that helped to determine that result.

The reader will not find here a comprehensive look at all that took place in Arkansas. As in any community, the unique events and the distinctive experiences that give meaning to the history of each individual are practically infinite. Some of these may be immensely important in themselves. This study, however, seeks to discover the larger themes that provide the framework for the Arkansas experience.

Arkansas and the New South
1874–1929

Arkansas Faces a New Era

In 1875 Arkansas emerged from fourteen years of turmoil when Congress voted to recognize Augustus H. Garland as the victor in the previous year's disputed gubernatorial election. Garland's assumption of power ended an upheaval marked by four years of war and nine years of Reconstruction. Many contemporary Arkansans believed that the Garland administration would establish a framework of political stability within which the state's resources would be developed and its people would prosper once again. Some even dared to hope that a "New Arkansas" would emerge upon the ruins of the old. The formula for success included the restoration of traditional commercial agriculture to its prewar levels of production, the invigoration of the farm economy through product diversification, and ultimately, the development of a supplemental manufacturing sector in the state.

During the fifty-four years prior to the Great Depression, Arkansans tried desperately to improve conditions within the state. In their attempt to bring the state within the nation's economic mainstream, they were like others across the region who envisioned an economic revolution that would produce what commonly was referred to as the "New South." At times, economic conditions suggested progress was being made toward this goal. Social and cultural changes also indicated that circumstances within the state were being transformed. In the end, they failed to achieve the radical changes that many hoped for in 1875. Still, what was accomplished drastically altered the Arkansas that had existed at the end of Reconstruction. While not the world they envisioned, it was nonetheless new. To get there, Arkansans experienced some five decades marked by individual initiative and struggle, volatile economic transformation, and social change and conflict.

The optimism for the future held by many Arkansans, especially whites but also some African Americans, at the end of Reconstruction originated in many different circumstances. Since political turmoil appeared to have ended, many thought that returning stability would encourage economic development. In addition, by 1875 the economic panic that had engulfed the nation in 1873 appeared to have run its course. Investment capital was once again available and prices for wholesale goods, especially agricultural products, had stabilized. The state's transportation system had been expanded with the advent of the railroads and the basic skeleton of a statewide system. All in all, the time seemed ripe for growth.

This new confidence infected individuals throughout the state, although it was articulated most vigorously and loudly by the members of Arkansas's relatively small business community. These individuals constituted a complex social group. Men from the north and foreign immigrants worked with Southern- and Arkansas-born citizens. Former Confederate soldiers cooperated with their Federal counterparts. Capitalist, industrialist, and planter joined as New South idealists. Among the most vocal spokesmen for this cause were newspapermen such as William E. Woodruff Jr., who had guided the *Arkansas Gazette* immediately following the war until 1876, and James Mitchell, who afterward edited both the *Gazette* and the *Arkansas Democrat*.

Those Arkansans who wanted to be part of a New South, however, found their hopes challenged by the existence of a local economy and a society that resisted all change. Agriculture committed largely to the production of a single crop dominated the economy, consuming capital and limiting efforts at diversification. In rural communities, social institutions and government organized people to ensure the operations of the farm economy, but at the same time stood as obstacles to innovation. If a New South was to be created, Arkansans not only had to overcome economic barriers but the limits of society as well.

The economic system that defined Arkansas in 1875, upon which the basic wealth of the state rested, and that proved so resistant to change was tied almost totally to agriculture. In 1870, census estimates indicated that the value of farm products accounted for over 93 percent of the total value of farm and manufacturing goods produced in the state. Capital invested in farming represented over 97 percent of the total agricultural and manufacturing investment statewide. Most of the people at work in the state labored on farms or were part of the commercial community that provided services for the agricultural population. Over 97 percent of the state's residents were considered rural.

By the 1870s the vast majority of Arkansas's farms had a commercial purpose; few remained that aimed merely at subsistence. The commercial farm raised a product that could be sold for cash at market. The extent to which the individual devoted resources to a commercial product varied according to factors such as the fertility of the land and the accessibility of transportation, but the aim invariably was to make enough money to get ahead, and that required producing something that could be sold. In the search for cash income the Arkansas farmer faced limits. The product that had the greatest value throughout this period was cotton, which sold in national and international markets to the textile manufacturers of Europe and of the northeastern United States. Farmers who grew wheat and other grains, hay, fruits or vegetables; dairymen; or stockmen and herders who raised animals for sale had access to more limited local and regional markets, and in these both demand and price fluctuated greatly.

Geographic conditions played a major role in determining whether farmers turned to cotton or developed other marketable crops or products. Where land was fertile and transportation to markets available, cotton was the inevitable choice of most. Where land was poorer or where access to national markets was more difficult, farmers had to be content with producing whatever they could for the local market. Geographical lines tended to divide the state into two major agricultural systems—the lowlands and river valleys devoted to the culture of cotton, and the uplands devoted to other agricultural goods. A line drawn from the northeastern corner of the state to the southwestern corner was the rough boundary, although not a precise one, between these two systems.

Farms varied according to the crops produced, but they also differed by the method of operation employed, particularly regarding the nature of labor that was used. Two major types of units typified the state's farms, both in the cotton and noncotton regions. The 1880 census indicated that the majority of farms within the state, almost 70 percent, were cultivated by the person who owned the land. The other type was operated by a tenant who worked someone else's land. In 1880 the majority of tenant farms were in the lowlands, particularly in the old plantation areas of the state. The proportion of tenants to actual landowners ranged as high as 77 percent in Crittenden County, with other cotton counties ranging over 60 percent. Despite its concentration in the old plantation region, however, tenantry existed throughout the state.

Understanding the tenant system is to perceive how the existing agricultural order limited the creation of greater economic diversity within the state. Tenant contracts varied. There were some cash renters, leasing lands in 1880 that varied in price from $1.50 per acre in upland areas of Dallas County to $10 per acre for improved tracts in the Mississippi River Delta. The majority, however, farmed on shares, using a system that had emerged in the plantation regions of the state in the years immediately following the Civil War as a response to market forces and as a resolution to the differing demands of landowners and former slaves. Whatever the specific financial arrangement, the landowner wanting a crop that was easily marketed typically specified in the contract that the tenant would grow cotton. These arrangements usually called for the sharecropper to provide the labor while the renter provided the land, farm animals, equipment, seed, and perhaps even a house and furniture. When the crop was harvested, the landowner received as much as one-half of the cotton and one-third of the corn in payment. The tenant received the rest.

The financing of both owner- and tenant-operated farms rested on a system of credit known as the crop-lien, which also compelled farmers to devote their resources to producing a cash crop for market. Credit was critical to the farmer, since he had to buy supplies at the beginning of each year with no promise of an income until the crop was sold at market at the end of the season. Often lacking savings to make such purchases, the farmer invariably borrowed money to start the year. In the antebellum years, farmers had often put up the value of their slaves or their land as collateral. After the war, slaves no longer existed and the value of land had collapsed, so the only property of any value held by most farmers was their crop. As a result, they used it as security against the loan, giving the creditor a lien (or the legal right) to the crop insuring payment of the debt.

The source of credit for most tenants was the landowner, usually backed by merchants in the major market towns. Additional credit was often provided by country merchants, who sold goods and even advanced cash against the tenant's share of the future crop (an arrangement known locally as the "truck system"). The country merchants were also the primary funding source for the small landowning farmer.

Creditors profited in this system by charging interest on the money they advanced and by securing the right to market the farmer's crop. Their role in directing the local economy was large. Wishing to secure the loans with a readily marketable commodity, creditors generally insisted that the farmer plant cotton. For those who wanted to put more land in food crops or to experiment with new products in the hopes of diversifying, credit was not as easy to obtain. Thus, the merchants controlled, within limits, what crops the system produced and how much land was devoted to particular crops. Credit, as the local newspapers often complained, played a major part in swaying Arkansans to devote so much of their energy to the production of cotton as their principal cash crop.

Determining the profitability of this system for Arkansans in 1880 is difficult. The situation of each individual farmer varied greatly over the state at any time, but for most in 1880 cotton farming was a risky enterprise. In that year a family of five, with four members fully committed to working fields, could have cultivated about thirty-two acres of cotton. In a good year on average land, this would have produced a crop for market of about sixteen bales (eight thousand pounds), after 10 percent of the harvest had been used to pay for ginning. If they could have received the New Orleans or Memphis market price of twelve cents per pound, which most small operators could not, that would have brought in $960 at the end of the year. For a tenant, half of this would have to go to the landowner, leaving $480 for a year's labor.

While farm income is relatively easy to calculate, the cost of farming and the cost of living that this income was measured against is more difficult to determine. The Department of Agriculture estimated the cost of growing a crop of eight thousand pounds of cotton in 1880 to range from $400 to $680. Department of Labor estimates of the cost of living for laboring families in 1900, which were roughly the same as in 1880, showed that a family of five in the South might spend as much as $292 on food alone during a year. Any other expenses, ranging from clothing to medicine, drove the cost of living further upward. Even though such measures are only approximations, the sum of the cost of production and the cost of living on a family cotton farm indicates how close income was to expense and how easily the landowning farm family could sink into debt. For the tenant family, the prospects were even more bleak.

With the promise of profits always so unpredictable, most farmers tried to ensure success by cutting expenses as much as possible. Thus, farmers were most resistant to consuming the goods that became available in stores in the late nineteenth century and tried, as best they could, to produce as much food and clothing on the farm as possible. If a farm could be self-sufficient, profits were more likely. Unfortunately for most, self-sufficiency was only an ideal. Some necessities could not be produced on the farm and had to be purchased: coffee, sugar, and salt were among these essentials. While many articles of clothing might be made at home, overalls and shoes were usually purchased. Blacksmith services, particularly repairs to equipment that could not be done on the farm, demanded money. Taxes were perhaps the most unavoidable cost that required the farmer to have cash. With the expansion of markets later in the century, temptations grew to purchase the many new goods that became available. A farm family had the potential for making money in 1880, but many variables had to fall into place for that to be accomplished. Without profits, farmers had few opportunities to change their lives.

In the end, agriculture was not just an economic system. It was a force that helped to define a way of life. Basic social and political institutions were closely connected to the agricultural economy and ensured the stability and order in the rural communities necessary for agrarian operations. For most of the 802,525 Arkansans who lived in the state in 1880, these institutions were central to their day-to-day existence. In that same year some 96 percent of the state's residents were considered rural, living either in the countryside or in villages with less than twenty-five-hundred persons. Statistics showing population density, that is, how many people on average lived within a square mile, confirmed this rural character. In 1880 Arkansas had only 15.1 persons per square mile, compared with 20.7 in neighboring Louisiana, 24.4 in Mississippi, and 31.6 in Missouri.

For these rural people, day-to-day life centered primarily on activities taking place on isolated farms. While Arkansans might make contact with the wider world at a crossroads village with its country store or church, they seldom saw or participated in the life of the larger town. Farmers commonly went to the county seat or to a larger community only twice a year: first, to secure credit and procure supplies in the spring, and then to sell crops, pay taxes, and buy winter provisions in the fall. Except for the head of the household, such trips might be even less frequent. Life involved contact with few persons other than family members and the closest neighbors. For these people, three major social institutions became central to life—family, class, and race. Each of these helped define the lives of rural folks. They also sustained the status quo and served as checks to change.

Family, often extending beyond the nuclear unit and at times even including servants and laborers, was clearly the most important social organization. It not only filled conventional biological and educational functions, but the family was also the primary economic unit in the agricultural economy. Every member had an important role as a farm laborer and was essential to ensuring the economic survival of the whole.

The problems associated with farm life meant that survival in the countryside was difficult for single men or women. Economic success practically required marriage, and the process of getting ahead almost always began with finding a spouse and having children. A young man who wanted to be on his own, free of his parents, not only needed land but labor, and a wife and children gave him that start. As a result, marriages tended to take place early. It was not uncommon for boys to be married by the age of seventeen and girls by sixteen. Romance probably helped partners select one another, but necessity often drove them together. Working side by side, young couples often made their first crop together, taking the first step toward their own economic autonomy and establishing the basis for their future.

Economic need, plus high infant mortality rates, encouraged couples to have large families. Prior to the development of modern medicine, many children did not survive to adulthood, which threatened the continued existence of the family line. Equally important, however, was that children provided the principal labor force on many farms, and more children meant greater agricultural productivity. In 1880 the average size of an Arkansas family was 5.2 people, a figure that does not reflect the actual number of childbirths within a household. This was not unlike family size throughout the United States at this time, although more urbanized and industrialized communities began to experience the development of smaller families. In Massachusetts, for example, a family in 1880 averaged only 4.7 people.

Accepted social traditions plus the nature of farm work defined gender- and age-specific roles for various family members. The normal family was considered one in which the father played the dominant role in matters related to the outside world and the final judge in domestic concerns as well. Men traditionally directed the farm work, which involved an enormous commitment of energy. In 1875 on the farm of George Boddie, a fifty-four-year-old farmer located in the Ouachita River bottoms north of Camden, the agricultural year began with the spring planting of corn, wheat, and some vegetables in early April and cotton at the end of the month. By June, Boddie, his family, and what workers he could hire were chopping cotton, plowing the corn to get rid of weeds, and planting vegetables such as peas. In July he had to harvest the wheat, while the cotton still required plowing to clear it of weeds. By late August, Boddie was in the field picking cotton, a task that continued through early December, then commenced harvesting corn by mid-October, planting winter wheat in November, and slaughtering hogs in November and December. Around January 1876, Boddie ginned his cotton, hauled it to nearby Camden, and personally supervised its sale. In addition to these numerous tasks associated with the farm's products, Boddie and his family built fences, repaired and built other structures, and attended to numerous jobs necessary to keep his farm running.

Women's work ordinarily revolved around the domestic or household economy. Tasks such as food preparation, which in the nineteenth century still included slaughtering small animals; growing, gathering, and preserving fruits and vegetables; as well as the actual cooking of foods; consumed large amounts of time. A woman's work even included tending to the garden and the chickens and pigs that would become the family's food. Washing was an arduous task that involved carrying water, boiling clothes in a large kettle heated by firewood, hand rubbing each garment to get out dirt, and then rinsing the wash before hanging it out to dry. On most farms, women still were responsible for making their own soap. While more and more clothing was purchased during this era and weaving cloth had been practically abandoned, most households still produced their own socks and underwear and women frequently fashioned dresses out of store-bought fabric. All this, in addition to child rearing, was the province of the farm woman.

The boundaries of women's lives extended outside of the household and into the surrounding neighborhood at times. When they could get away from home chores, neighborhood women assisted each other through many of life's crises. They gathered to assist each other in childbirth, providing assistance and support at a time when doctors were seldom present for that event. Women often sat with the dying and then took charge of the burial rituals for the dead, offering not only a practical service but comfort for those left behind. In these ways women helped create a world apart from the men.

In the farm family, childhood as a special phase of life different from adulthood lasted for only a short time. By the age of five or six, children were expected to help their father or their mother in their tasks. Boys took care of milking cows, feeding animals, and ultimately went to the fields with their fathers. Girls learned homemaking skills and assisted in rearing younger children in the family. The time of childhood and play passed quickly, replaced by practical education. In the course of assisting with chores on the farm and in the household they learned the tasks appropriate to their sex and necessary for them to perform adult duties in their own family in the future. In addition to learning these critical skills, they also contributed to the family's well-being through their work.

These patterns represented what was considered a normal role for family members, but actual situations required flexibility. Real families rarely resembled the ideal. The role of women was particularly susceptible to change. Injuries, illness, death, or even the inability of a husband to do what was expected often forced a wife to assume traditional male roles. At critical times during the year, particularly at harvest time or if a family did not have access to labor, women were expected to work in the fields alongside the men. A community's definitions of the proper role for a man and a woman gave way quickly in the face of need.

Economic endeavors consumed much of the time of rural family members, but the family provided the framework for other activities as well. Much of the education of children took place within the household as children worked with their parents in carrying out farm tasks. For a young person who intended to remain on the farm, there was actually little need for the classical knowledge that formed the basis of traditional schools. Basic reading and writing skills and the ability to do simple arithmetic were important, but beyond these capabilities little formal education was necessary. Statistics for the 1880s and 1890s showed generally that in the countryside only about 50 percent of school-aged children ever went to school, a figure equally applicable to both whites and blacks. Entries in biographical dictionaries in the late nineteenth and early twentieth centuries testify again and again to the success of the young farmers with only a minimum of formal education but the ability to learn from experience.

As in the case of education, the rural community's entertainment and leisure activities were informal and often took place within the family. Play for children consisted of simple activities, usually with brothers and sisters or with other children from the immediate neighborhood, and their play often mimicked adult activities. Boys quickly made the transition from homemade slingshots that could be used to kill small birds and animals to guns that could be used to bring in extra food for the family. Among adults, visiting was one of the principal forms of entertainment. Neighborhood women called upon one another, sharing surplus goods and each other's company. Men also visited, although usually when at market or on court day. While communities at times engaged in more formal leisure activities such as a church picnic or even a revival, these were not frequent occurrences.

To the outsider who visited the countryside, rural life and society appeared remarkable in its sameness. The common endeavor of farm families and the acceptance of a narrowly defined set of behaviors and values considered normal made it appear that most rural peoples were much alike. In fact, this was not true. Underneath the similarities lay marked differences created by wealth and race. Everyone farmed, their lifestyles were similar, but everyone was not equal. Among whites—in addition to family—class and race were major institutions providing the individual with an identity.

The class system that existed presented no clear lines marking one level of society from another, but people at the time understood that there were differences. Although her perceptions of the system's dynamics were romantic, Alice French, a late-nineteenth-century author who lived at Clover Bend plantation in Lawrence County and wrote under the pseudonym Octave Thanet, was one of the many who saw local rural white society divided into three classes: the wealthy, the independent and solid yeomanry, and the poor rustics. These divisions were pervasive throughout the state.

By the 1870s and 1880s rural elites were in the process of considerable change. Wealthy landowning planters and merchants still maintained control over vast regions of the countryside, but increasingly these people opted to live away from the land they owned. They might maintain a country house, but through most of the year the family resided in a nearby town or even in the larger cities. While their wealth came from the countryside, they spent their lives in an urban culture. Ultimately, they became culturally more urban than rural.

The largest portion of the population were those white farmers who operated either medium sized or small farms and who owned their own land or were buying it. Successful white tenants might even be considered a part of this class. In 1880 this amounted to approximately 70 percent of the total white farm population statewide. Their numbers varied regionally, however. In an area with large plantations such as Phillips County, this independent landowning class constituted only 34 percent of the population.

In Benton County in northwestern Arkansas, far from the plantation, it accounted for some 82 percent.

The lifestyle of the yeoman class was considered the ideal. With fewer financial emergencies, these families could maintain gender- and age-role differentiation among its members. Men could devote their attention to the outside world while women could remain engaged in domestic economy. Childhood and the absence of responsibility could be retained longer for middle-class children, which meant that most had greater opportunities to attend school. Economic crises could change these relationships, but a landed farmer generally possessed the means to keep the family in its proper order.

The prosperous farm family also was recognizable by its material possessions. Some visitors to Arkansas during this period were surprised to discover that the yeoman's home often was filled with the same goods that could be found in rural households throughout the nation. They purchased many goods that they previously would have produced on the farm—particularly clothing and some prepared foods. While they held much in common with poorer farm families, the yeoman class were ultimately marked by their distinctive lifestyle and their material possessions.

At the bottom, at least as perceived by those above them, was a lower class consisting of tenants and laborers. They were, in short, the landless members of rural society. This group steadily increased throughout the late nineteenth century as economic conditions worsened and came to represent a larger and larger segment of both the white and the total population. The more successful members of the community considered the landless not only poor but also possessing unique class characteristics. Terms applied to them, such as "poor whites," "white trash," "rednecks," or in the mountains, "hillbillies," were loaded with meaning and suggested that this class was not only poor but also lazy and uncouth—they brought poverty upon themselves through their behavior. The "Arkansas Traveler," a stereotype created in the early nineteenth century for Arkansas mountain people, possessed the character flaws attributed to poor white Arkansans for years to come.

Life for these people was often very hard. Economic survival was never certain. As a result, traditional definitions of gender roles within the family tended to break down. The poor farm family had to exploit the labor of every member, children and women usually worked in the fields alongside the men throughout the year. For the women this was particularly hard since field work did not relieve them from the responsibility of the household as well. Alice French, again writing of society in Lawrence County, observed that a high price was paid. Working both in the home and in the fields, she concluded, "They [women] age early and die, when under happier chances they would be in their prime."

Some observers found little tension existing between these various classes. In the late 1870s this may have been so. Small farmers could still hope to make a fortune and move up in society, which may have undermined the development of serious class conflict. Individual cases of upward mobility reinforced this belief. While an improved position never occurred for most, the possibility existed and was enough for even the poorest tenant to embrace the system. Events during the 1880s, however, tended to shatter this dream as well as the social peace and make white Arkansans even more aware of the economic differences that divided them.

Rural Arkansans were also divided along lines of race. African-Americans lived in a world to themselves. They constituted some 26 percent of the total population of the state, although in some of the older plantation counties their numbers were greater. In Chicot County, for example, African-Americans constituted 85 percent of the population. Alice French's recognition that poor whites were convinced that they were no man's inferior, and "every black man's superior," defined the basic racial attitude of all whites. Black Arkansans were permanently at the bottom of society in the eyes of whites and constituted a perpetual work force for the plantations and farms of the state.

White racism, which asserted that African-Americans were inferior as a people, was based on generally contradictory observations. Blacks were seen as rowdy, uneducable, and lazy. At the same time, whites assumed that blacks were well fitted for work in the fields and worked hard so long as they were not tampered with by outsiders or educators. Whites recognized that all African-Americans did not fit their stereotype of the race, but they did not let their awareness of individual differences prevent them from making gross assumptions about blacks.

The lifestyle of the majority of African-Americans was not appreciably different from that of lower-class whites. Both lived in a world of grinding poverty that virtually denied them a chance to get ahead, relegating them to an almost permanent place at the bottom of society. Life always existed on the margin for both poor whites and blacks. Survival was never assured. The simple lack of material goods, as with poor whites, reflected the depth of their poverty. Scott Bond, an African-American who would personally escape the poverty of the countryside, recalled that when he and his wife settled on a tenant farm near Forrest City in the 1870s, their possessions included a barn door turned over a flour barrel for a table, soap boxes for chairs, and nothing else. For cooking they had only one pot, an iron tea kettle, that had to be used for cooking and cleaning.

Although whites lumped all African-Americans together, class differentiation may have existed to some extent within black society. Little is known of the dynamics of such a system however. A few African-Americans did achieve economic success. Scott Bond rose from tenant farmer to landowner in St. Francis County, and by the time he was sixty owned twenty-one farms and five cotton gins in the vicinity of Wittsburg and Madison. This made little difference in how whites viewed him, though. Bond realized that he could not cross the race line and, rather than provoke conflict, insisted that whites address him as "uncle" rather than "mister."

In the countryside the line between the races was clear and any step across it was dangerous. Violence was a common means by which whites asserted their own superiority with little fear of retribution. Blacks, on the other hand, had little means of replying. When a black tenant farmer was taken out by unknown parties and flogged for neglecting his crops, as was done near Magnolia in 1889, the lesson about the relative power of one race to the other was made clear without any formal or institutional statements.

Family, class, and race were the core of rural social existence, but a variety of more formal institutions touched upon the lives of rural Arkansans as well. Carrying out specialized functions, particularly offering ideas that justified and legalized the values of the rural world, church and government were the two most important of these institutions. Providing support for the existing system, they often worked as major barriers to innovations that threatened to produce change.

Churches obviously played a major role in rural Arkansas, as in other cultures, providing meaning within an incomprehensible world and relieving the anxiety of living. Relative to the state's plight in the 1870s, however, churches also played a role in supporting the social world of family, class, and race that existed.

Churches generally were associated with major denominations that existed throughout the state and nation. Most of these in Arkansas, nearly 80 percent, were Baptist or Methodist and were largely self-governing congregations. Lacking larger hierarchical organizations, without formally trained clergies, and with budgets and pastors' salaries in the hands of the membership, these churches seldom represented the presence of an outside force in the community. At least on most social issues, they reflected the dominant attitudes of the neighborhood. The social content of religion tended to reaffirm local values.

Theological disputes were heated and delineated differences among these various congregations. There might even be some disagreements over the specific meaning of the Gospels when applied to local society. On the whole, however, the social doctrine advanced in these churches emphasized values designed to stabilize the community, actively seeking the suppression of behaviors that might undermine the public peace. Drunkenness, sexual transgressions, profanity, or lying, all of which threatened community order, were central concerns. Deterring these behaviors was particularly important as they threatened to introduce conflict among community members and to undermine the stability of the family, the most critical social unit to the community's existence.

The church had real power to force individuals to conform in rural communities. Most congregations typically held monthly meetings to discuss business and also to consider what was called the "peace of the church," which involved the scrutinizing of suspect members and disciplining those who had strayed. If the accused failed to be acquitted or would not admit to sin, the church would hand down a letter of dismissal, the stigma of which carried potentially dire secular consequences. The dismissed member would often be shunned by other Christians in community life, making survival difficult where most residents of an area belonged to the same church. One's options were either to start another church, which was not easy in a small town, or to leave. Usually such measures were unnecessary, for the member admitted to un-Christian conduct and the congregation offered forgiveness. Whatever the result, however, equilibrium within the community was ensured.

While religion dealt with the supernatural basis for authority and provided a moral explanation for the exercise of power in the community, government and the law provided the secular vehicle for the same end. In form, government was democratic in nature, but assumptions about who should participate restricted the actual working of democracy. Individual power and authority were primarily the possession of adult men, particularly white men. The 1874 Constitution put forward this idea clearly when it declared every "male citizen" of the age of twenty-one was entitled to vote. In the wake of Reconstruction this included African-American men, but racist attitudes denied real equality or meaningful participation in the political process to that group except in certain particular locales.

Public policies provide the best insight into the interests that dominated government. For most people the work of the county courts, the justices of the peace, and the officials of the local judiciary had the most direct relevance to day-to-day life. The county courts consisted of an elected judge sitting with the justices of the peace. These courts were particularly powerful in local matters, given exclusive jurisdiction by the state constitution in matters related to county taxes; maintenance of roads, bridges, and ferries; taking care of paupers, bastardy, vagrants, and the apprenticeship of minors; and disbursement of monies. A clause giving it responsibility for all other matters necessary for internal improvements and for local concerns of the county was similar to the "necessary and proper" clause of the national constitution in opening up the possibility of even broader powers.

The justices also were important individually. They had original jurisdiction in contract disputes not exceeding one hundred dollars and concurrent jurisdiction with the circuit courts in contract disputes up to three hundred dollars. They also sat in judgment of suits to recover personal property up to three hundred dollars and to secure redress in cases involving damages to personal property of up to one hundred dollars. Justices of the peace also heard those misdemeanor cases assigned to them by law and were able to hold hearings, practically acting as a grand jury.

While the personnel of county government generally reflected the broader local population, the policies invariably mirrored the interests of wealth and property, bolstering their prerogatives and sustaining their needs. Taxes were low, with the actual tax rate in 1880 set at .008 cent on the assessed dollar, below the constitutional limit of .010 cent. School district taxes, capped by the constitution at .005 cent were actually .003 cent, a rate about one-third of those in the New England and Midwestern states at this time. Assessments were also generally low, further ensuring a small tax burden for propertied interests. The dockets of the courts considered disputes between landowners and tenants, invariably finding in favor of landowners. The county justices also maintained social order, particularly family stability, considering issues such as disturbing the peace and public disputes between married couples. More to the point, they enforced public morality, prosecuting individuals charged with gambling, prostitution, breaking Sabbath laws, living together without being married, or breaking racial laws prohibiting whites and blacks from being married.

The majority of rural Arkansans probably did not see the impact of state government on their lives as directly as local government, but the policies of officials in Little Rock provided a further bulwark for the power of white landowners. From 1874 and into the twentieth century, the Democratic Party dominated the political landscape and determined these policies. The remnants of the Republican Party and a variety of third parties challenged this domination at times, but the Democrats never lost control of the governor's office or the legislature.

On the surface the Democrats appeared to be a fractious coalition, with disputes over policy and leadership always present. Despite these squabbles, however, the Democratic Party clearly represented the landed interests of the state. In many ways they were an extension of the power of the ante-bellum elite. The first post-Reconstruction governor, Augustus H. Garland, had been a prominent lawyer prior to the Civil War, a member of the secession convention, a representative in the Confederate Congress, and an ardent supporter of the Confederacy. Although Garland had been a Whig before the war rather than a Democrat, his election and his subsequent course as governor indicated clearly the return to power of the old propertied interests within the state. Garland was followed by a series of governors who also showed the continuing connection of post-Reconstruction politics with pre-war and wartime politics and the same inactive approach to government: William R. Miller, Confederate state auditor, was elected in 1876 and 1878. Thomas J. Churchill, a planter and Confederate major general, secured the office in 1880. James H. Berry, a Confederate veteran who had lost a leg at Corinth, was elected in 1882. Simon P. Hughes, a planter and Confederate officer, won in 1884 and then again in 1886. James P. Eagle of Lonoke County won the office in 1888 and 1890. The election of William M. Fishback, a wartime Unionist, in 1892 appeared to break this trend, but Fishback had made his peace with the Democratic majority while serving in the legislature in the 1880s when he attempted to prohibit state authorities from paying for various bonds that had been issued during Reconstruction.

Rather than the governors, however, the Democratic candidates elected to the Constitutional Convention of 1874 and to subsequent state legislatures reflected more clearly the importance of agrarian interests in politics, playing a critical role in advancing and executing policy favorable to this elite. Their 1874 constitution severely restricted the powers of the state government and decentralized power, returning critical authority to county and municipal governments, invariably controlled by local landed and commercial interests. Among the actions of the state convention (which met from July 4 through September 8) were measures that seriously restricted the powers of the governor, especially by reducing the term of office from four to two years and by cutting appointment powers. In addition, the delegates constrained the ability of the government to tax by capping the maximum taxes allowed by both state and county governments, prohibiting the loaning of credit or the issuing of any interest-bearing bonds, warrants, or scrip, except to service the already existing debt, and limiting salaries of officials.

The Twentieth General Assembly, which met from November 1874 to March 1875, solidified what was referred to sometimes as the Bourbon Revolution. Like the French Royalists who had restored Bourbon kings to the throne of France in 1815, local Bourbons returned the state's old landed elite to power. The legislative program focused on their concerns, particularly in establishing control and limits over taxation. One of the most critical acts of the legislature was to place assessment of property in the hands of locally elected assessors, removing this power from those appointed by the governor as stipulated by the constitution of 1868. This practically ensured that local agricultural interests would be able to control their tax burden by limiting assessments. The results of this change in practice were reflected immediately as property assessments lowered throughout the state.

The legislature showed a desire to significantly limit any taxes, levying little more than half of the total allowed by the new constitution. In addition to a state poll tax, the legislature levied a six-mill property tax to support the state government, to pay the interest on the public debt, and to support common schools. Counties were prohibited from raising taxes of more than fifteen mills: five for general purposes, five to pay county debts, and five for schools. Towns and cities were limited to no more than ten mills.

Each new legislature that followed the inauguration of this new era in 1875 pursued a policy of fiscal conservatism and limited action by the state government. Taxes were reduced and efforts at expanding public services were rebuffed. Statistics gathered by the Federal government showed that ad valorem taxes in Arkansas had been $3.03 per $100 valuation in 1870, compared to $0.35 in 1860. The legislature reduced the tax rate to $2.13 by 1880, and then dropped it to $1.61 in 1890. During the 1890s, the rate climbed back to as high as $1.98, but the basic trend toward lower taxes was clear.

The 1875 General Assembly also set the fundamental pattern within which the legislature would deal with labor issues in the state. In a crop-lien law and an act to regulate the labor system, the legislature upheld the right of lien holders against a tenant's share of the crop. However, tenants received no legal protections against the fraud of merchants and landowners who might prey upon them.

A consensus on the need for lower tax rates and assessments did not mean that there was complete agreement among Democrats on fiscal matters. Many Bourbons were particularly concerned with the outstanding indebtedness of the state left over from the war and Reconstruction. Servicing these debts demanded continued taxation, but this ran counter to Bourbon goals. The easiest way to have handled these debts and allowed further tax cuts would have been to repudiate them. Repudiation of legitimate debts, however, would have destroyed the state's credit and its ability to borrow in the future. The debt issue exposed some of the differences that existed within the Democratic Party at the time: agricultural interests saw no reason to honor the debt and were willing to repudiate it, but business and commerce viewed this as a threat to state credit and its ability to support the growth of transportation.

The relative power of the two groups within the party clarified when the agrarians moved to repudiate parts of the debt, and the other wing could do little but delay the final results. They focused on the legitimacy of legislation from 1868, when the general assembly passed a controversial measure fully funding what were known as the "Holford Bonds" and other issues for railroad and levee construction. At the risk of losing state credit, in 1879 the pro-agriculture legislators in the general assembly tried to secure a constitutional amendment prohibiting the levying of taxes or the use of state appropriations to pay for these bonds. They failed in this attempt, but a second amendment was introduced and passed in 1884. The strength of the agrarian interests within the party was clear in the election results, with 119,806 voters favoring the repudiation amendment while only 15,492 voted against it.

Arkansas's government essentially adopted a pay-as-you-go philosophy and constantly sought ways of cutting costs within traditional government programs. Typical of the institutions that emerged during the Redeemer era was the prisoner-lease system, by which legislators intended that the state prisons become self-financing through the work of inmates. The system had been initiated during Reconstruction, and Redeemer governments continued to lease prisoners to private contractors. Little effort was made to regulate the treatment of these inmates until 1883, when the state prescribed rules for the use of prisoners—binding the lessees to limit convict labor to ten hours per day and to provide sufficient and wholesome food. The 1883 law, at the same time, extended the lease system to county prisoners but did little to prevent continued abuse of convict laborers. Particular problems developed in the western Arkansas coal mines, which hired hundreds of prison laborers. An investigating committee in 1888 reported that workers received minimum rations, little clothing, and harsh whippings if they did not bring in daily allotments of coal. While the issue of convict leases became the subject of increasing criticism through the late nineteenth century, little change took place. Another legislative effort at changing the system in 1893 simply replaced the existing system with a contract-lease system, and convicts continued to be hired out for everything from railroad construction to domestic service.

From 1875 through the next century, the Bourbons maintained control over state government and used it, as best they could, to protect themselves in an economically insecure era. In legislature after legislature and from governor to governor, the Bourbons left a legacy of minimum government and low taxes to the people of Arkansas, government that provided few services, but that at the same time reinforced the peculiar economic position of the old propertied elite within the state.

Despite the problems connected with Redeemer government, these men, based on the rural power structures in Arkansas, effectively held on to control of the state government through the end of the nineteenth century. They faced increasing opposition from a variety of discontented elements within the state, but none of these ever successfully overturned their power. Ultimately, the political legacy they created provided a restrictive framework which seriously limited the future of the state and hindered efforts by those who envisioned a more rapid pace of development.

Individual Arkansans may have hoped for changes after 1874, but conditions in the state presented enormous barriers. An economic system in which most institutions pushed labor into agricultural pursuits, a society that offered few alternative visions, and institutions that reinforced the status quo worked together as powerful impediments to change. Remarkably, however, change did take place.

Forces of Change

———————⟡———————

In the years after 1875, Arkansas's economy grew, despite the serious obstacles in the way. Progress was made toward the goals of the New South advocates, particularly in efforts at developing economic sectors other than agriculture. The state's natural resources, largely undeveloped in 1875, were increasingly exploited. A manufacturing sector, although remaining relatively small, showed spectacular growth and promise for the future. From the end of Reconstruction through the turn of the century, significant economic changes took place that marked the first stage of what some Arkansans hoped would be a new prosperity.

The local businessmen and entrepreneurs who worked for economic development approached the problem using the same model that had been used elsewhere in the nation throughout the century. They first had to attract private investment capital to the state in order to build the railroads necessary to integrate the local economy regionally and nationally. Then they must promote the agricultural economy, which would develop the state's natural resources and generate the local wealth that would build the factories essential to economic diversification. These men believed that the state offered businessmen many natural advantages, especially its resources and its location along new routes of transportation, but they also assumed that government had to provide an attractive environment for the investor.

The experiences of Reconstruction and the financial problems of the state government limited what they could do. Nonetheless, through the legislature the New South advocates secured what they could to attract immigrants and investors to the state.

The business developers of 1875 faced a major problem in using government to pursue their goals. A traditional means of encouraging economic investment, the use of state bonds either to finance or back private companies that might locate in the state, had been undermined by the Republican state government during Reconstruction. To encourage railroad, highway, and even levee construction, state and local governments had engaged in an unbridled issuing of bonds. By 1875 the ability of the state government to service its outstanding debts was uncertain, especially without higher taxes. Agrarian resistance to raising taxes meant that the state had reached its bonding limits, and outright financial support of private businesses that might locate in Arkansas was impossible.

At times the legislature did move cautiously in providing direct support for enterprises, particularly the development of transportation. Usually, however, the state allowed local authorities to control such efforts rather than becoming involved itself. Land forfeited for the nonpayment of taxes in the counties was allowed to be used to support the construction of railroads, but only in the county where the lands were located. Levee construction was encouraged and tax increases were authorized for this end, but the actual power to build the levees and to raise the taxes was placed in the hands of county courts and local levee districts.

With state government so reluctant to provide direct financing for economic activities, developers were forced to use other measures to attract investors. Article X of the state constitution allowed the general assembly to pass laws that would foster economic development, including tax exemptions for mining and manufacturing enterprises. The 1875 General Assembly passed such a law, typical of those used by many frontier states to attract investors. The legislation exempted from taxation for seven years capital of over two thousand dollars that was invested in mining and manufacturing, specifically cotton, woolen, or yarn mills; agricultural implements factories; tanneries; cottonseed-oil mills; and mining or smelting furnaces. The exemption allowed risk takers to reinvest profits as they began and required no cash outlays by the state. It cost the state initially by depriving it of taxes, but in the long run, at least theoretically, firmly established enterprises would produce larger and lasting revenues for the state.

The constitution also empowered the legislature to create the Mining, Manufacturing, and Agricultural Bureau and the office of state geologist to help publicize the state's economic opportunities. Under these provisions the general assembly created an immigration bureau in 1875, but it was never funded well and its directors relied on voluntary support from local communities to carry out its activities. J. N. Smithee was named first commissioner of immigration, but from the beginning both Smithee and his office was criticized as ineffective. His efforts attracted more farmers, but not the people the developers wanted to exploit the state's resources. The office was reconstituted in 1886 during the administration of Gov. Simon P. Hughes, but it still relied upon voluntary support for its budget and most of its activities. Government efforts at promoting economic development through such special agencies were generally ineffective throughout this era.

Developers found their hands tied by Arkansas's economic situation in 1875, but in many ways the state's support of development during Reconstruction had already put in place crucial elements that promoted the desired economic revolution. The issue of state bonds to finance railroad construction may have come close to bankrupting the government, but the policy had produced railroads, the key to economic change. Railroads were revolutionizing the way goods were produced and sold across the nation. They were breaking down local economies and integrating them into larger regional and national markets. Arkansas already had the skeleton of a railroad system in place at the end of Reconstruction, and the areas along the new rail lines were already linked to the emerging national market.

The actual development of the state's railroad system had begun prior to the Civil War. The legislature had given the Memphis and Little Rock Railroad Company the right to claim public lands offered by the federal government in 1853 to support the construction of a road from Cairo, Illinois, to Fulton, Arkansas, with branches to Fort Smith and to the Mississippi River. The state also appropriated its own funds to encourage development. The Civil War, however, halted construction with only a small segment of road completed between Little Rock and DeValls Bluff.

Efforts were renewed after the war. The 1867 passage of a law offering companies $10,000 for every mile of line constructed led to the formation of some eighty-six different companies trying to get a piece of the railroad-bond pie. Most of these never built a single mile of track and did not receive bond money, but the accomplishments of the successful companies were amazing. By April 1871 the Memphis and Little Rock was completed with the bridging of the White River at DeValls Bluff. In April 1872 the St. Louis, Iron Mountain, and Southern, building the mainline envisioned in the federal legislation of 1853, had regular service from Little Rock to St. Louis. In August 1873 the Iron Mountain had reached Fulton, bridged the Red River, and by the following January was at Texarkana. Slower to get started, by 1874 the Little Rock and Fort Smith had reached Van Buren, completing the western branch of the old Cairo and Fulton.

The completion of the old Cairo and Fulton's proposed lines established the basic rail network within the state and tied Arkansas directly to the new national railroad system. By the end of Reconstruction, backed with state bonds, the number of miles of track in operation within the state had increased from only thirty-eight miles to over seven hundred miles. The impact of the new transportation system was almost immediate. The time and cost it took to go somewhere or to ship goods dropped sharply. When Cornelia Dickson, a school teacher in Ouachita County, traveled from Camden to Selma, Alabama, in 1874, the first part of the trip was on a stage from Camden to Prescott. The stage took twelve and a half hours to cover forty miles and cost $6.40. Dickson got on the Iron Mountain train at Prescott and the eighty-two miles to Little Rock took three and a half hours and cost $4.50. While the train averaged twenty miles per hour, compared to the stage's three miles per hour, the price of transportation on the train had dropped to six cents per mile compared to sixteen cents per mile on the stage. It was no wonder that Arkansans like Cornelia Dickson felt like they were flying when they took the train and that a rapid increase in passenger and freight movement took place. The world of Arkansans had become significantly smaller.

The completion of the proposed Cairo and Fulton network was only the beginning of the state's railroad boom. During the latter part of the 1870s and then through the 1880s both branch lines and new mainlines proliferated. In part, the continued boom came as local communities did everything they could to secure a road that would tie them to the existing mainlines. Businessmen realized that such connections were critical. To fail to secure a rail link was to risk the economic future of their town. Camden was typical. A primary market for farmers all along the Ouachita River since antebellum times, the city found much of this trade diverted through Arkadelphia when the Iron Mountain reached that town in 1873. Struggling economically, Camden's businessmen gave the Iron Mountain $22,000 and provided the right of way along the entire route to encourage the construction of a branch that connected with the mainline at Gurdon. A line from the Iron Mountain at Malvern to Hot Springs, the Arkansas and Louisiana Railroad tying Indian Territory to the Iron Mountain at Hope, a road from Helena to the Memphis and Little Rock at Forrest City, and the Missouri and North Arkansas connecting the Iron Mountain to the St. Louis and San Francisco in Missouri were typical of the efforts by local businessmen to connect their communities with the rail system.

In addition to these various branch and independent feeder lines, the state benefited from a second wave of mainline railroad construction during the 1880s. This second boom resulted primarily from the efforts of business interests in St. Louis to connect a larger hinterland into their market. The first of these new lines was the St. Louis Southwestern Railroad, usually called the "Cotton Belt." The purpose of this road was to penetrate the agricultural areas in eastern and southern Arkansas. Out of Missouri the proposed route ran through Jonesboro, Clarendon, and on south through Stuttgart, Pine Bluff, Fordyce, Camden, and Texarkana. Much of this road was completed by the end of 1882. Another road promoted by business interests at St. Louis, the St. Louis and San Francisco, or "Frisco," entered the state at two different points. One route crossed the northeastern part of the state, connecting St. Louis with Memphis. The second passed through northwestern Arkansas, running through Rogers, Fayetteville, Van Buren, and Fort Smith. The Kansas City Southern, promoted by a rival city to St. Louis, pushed its route across western Arkansas, running through Benton County in the northwest, then into Oklahoma before reentering the state in Scott County and extending on to Texarkana.

By 1895 the rail network in the state was 2,373 miles long. These railroads had revolutionized transportation and, as their boosters had predicted, had changed basic economic patterns. There were still problems, though. The railroads themselves turned out to be powerful monopolies with which Arkansas business interests had to contend. While offering an alternative method of transportation to wagons and steamboats as well as lowered shipping rates, railroads did not provide the services or level of rate reduction that many had hoped. The roads did not compete with each other, and as a result many local communities found themselves totally dependent on virtual monopolies for their transportation. Merchants, happy at first to have the railroads come to their towns, began to complain particularly about shipping costs. When comparing short-haul rates in Arkansas to long-haul rates charged by railroads elsewhere, the businessmen concluded that the former were arbitrarily determined and ultimately discriminatory. Merchant protests, however, had little influence with the companies and, without alternative routes, local communities and their merchants had no other options for transportation in the new system.

Another cause for concern among some Arkansans was the power of the railroads to influence governmental policy. During the late 1870s, the public became increasingly concerned with the resistance of railroads to all efforts at taxing them or ensuring that their property was fairly assessed. Through the early 1880s the public placed increasing pressure on the general assembly to assert greater control over the railroads, particularly regarding property assessments and the gathering of state taxes from the companies. Ultimately, the 1883 General Assembly created a commission to assess the property of railroads rather than have the companies present their own assessment as had been done in the past. Although a small step, it was a first one toward ultimate regulation of the railroad companies.

There were problems, but most Arkansans were willing to overlook the difficulties. The new railroads had made it possible for local businesses to deal with other markets and, according to contemporary newspapers, had broken the almost monopolistic hold of New Orleans businessmen over the state, a source of complaint throughout the antebellum years. Memphis was the initial beneficiary as agricultural goods poured out of Arkansas along the Memphis and Little Rock line. The completion of the Cairo and Fulton, however, began to move trade toward St. Louis, leading to complaints from Memphis businessmen. While much produce continued to move east to Memphis and south to New Orleans, St. Louis increasingly became the economic center to which Arkansans turned both as a market for their goods and as the financial and wholesale center for the state's buyers.

The roads also appeared to have initiated the prosperity that everyone had expected of them, and they seemed to promise even greater economic growth. By 1877 the *Arkansas Gazette* reported a steady increase in the population and wealth of the state and pinpointed the areas of greatest activity as those made accessible by the railroads. A correspondent of the *Philadelphia Press* informed easterners in 1878 that the railroads, with two great lines intersecting the state at right angles, had given an "impetus to business and an improvement to the State, which marks the beginning of a new era in its history." He wrote, "I came to Arkansas expecting to see the worst country I had ever looked upon, and I certainly see the best."

Whether the opportunities created by the railroads or the favorable policies created by the state government were most attractive, by the late 1870s the state and its towns clearly were becoming places to invest in new enterprises and, consequently, were experiencing an economic boom. Visitors to Little Rock at this time discovered new manufacturing activities. Foundries, lumber and planing mills, flouring mills, and a cottonseed-oil mill were among the signs of change. Even though such industries were unsophisticated relative to those in the Northeast at this time, compared to what had existed within the state in the past the change was significant. In addition, commerce and trade flourished.

The entrepreneurs responsible for this growth came from a variety of backgrounds. Often the actual creators of the developing economy were not native to Arkansas. Newcomers to the state were particularly important in the development of the state's timber resources. Arkansas Lumber Company, headquartered at Warren and possessing some 70,000 acres of land, was owned by Moses Rittenhouse and John W. Embree of Chicago. Hovey and McCracken, the Bradley Lumber Company, and the Southern Lumber Company were among the other companies belonging to out-of-state interests. On the other hand, in many cases these outsiders cooperated with local capitalists. In the case of Little Rock's first cottonseed-oil mill, Edmund Urquhart of Canada worked with John G. Fletcher, a native-born Confederate veteran and banker, and Logan Roots, an Illinois-born Union veteran of Gen. William T. Sherman's staff and banker, in establishing the Little Rock Oil Company in 1875.

Among the earliest industrial activities made possible by the new conditions of the late 1870s was the exploitation of the state's natural resources. Arkansans had long believed that the state offered the potential investor a treasure house of raw materials. Timber and a variety of minerals were present in large quantities. Even the state's scenery was a potentially exploitable resource. Only a lack of access had delayed their full use and development. All of that changed when the railroads penetrated the countryside.

The beginning of a tourism industry was closely tied to railroad expansion. Tourism had significant long-term potential, but at least at the beginning its economic impact was largely a local one. Blessed with scenic countryside in the western mountains and with mineral springs believed to have curative powers, Arkansas had been a place that attracted visitors even before the Civil War. The railroads made all of these attractions even more accessible, however, and entrepreneurs expanded the facilities for tourists and went out of their way to attract them. In 1875 Hot Springs was tied to the mainline of the Iron Mountain Railroad at Malvern. Eureka Springs prospered after the completion in 1883 of the Eureka Springs Railway Company, led by Powell Clayton, connecting that town with the mainline of the Frisco Railroad twenty miles away at Seligman, Missouri. Almost overnight, Eureka Springs was transformed from a pine-lumber camp to a booming town known as the "Switzerland of America," at least in the local travel literature. Ultimately, the community had some one hundred hotels, including the handsome five-story stone-constructed Crescent, financed by Clayton. By the end of the nineteenth century, Eureka Springs and Hot Springs were both known across the nation as health resorts. Mount Nebo in the Ouachita Mountains developed as a resort to which city dwellers and people from the lowlands to the east and south could escape in the summer. The influx of tourists may have produced significant cultural changes in these areas, but little is known of what this might have been.

The exploitation of other natural assets proved financially more important, however. The growth of the lumber and timber industry was particularly significant, partly because of the wealth it generated but also because it was a statewide endeavor. Every region still possessed forest lands and was able to profit from this industry's expansion. The possibilities were obvious and potentially lucrative. In the 1870s observers estimated that the state's forests would last for several decades, and as late as 1900, after twenty years of timber harvesting, estimates indicated that some 84 percent of the total area of the state remained covered with trees. Hardwoods, particularly valuable as lumber, still constituted the bulk of these virgin forests. The richness of this resource was inestimable.

Cutting trees and sawing the logs into lumber was an important local enterprise almost from the beginning of the settlement of the state, but the market remained primarily local until the 1870s. In the eastern and southern parts of the state, river transportation made possible the exporting of some timber to markets in northern Louisiana and Mississippi, but the lack of adequate transportation left much of the state's forests unexploited. The building of the railroads meant that for the first time large-scale cutting and processing of timber was profitable and could claim a national market.

Entrepreneurs from throughout the nation moved to take advantage of this opportunity. Dozens of companies set up operations in almost every county of the state, acquiring rights to timber lands and developing mills for processing the harvest. Bluff City Lumber Company, Arkadelphia Lumber Company, Bradley Lumber, Sunny South, Southern, Gate City, Red River, Interstate, E. W. Frost, Bodcaw, Neimeyer, Sawyer-Austin, and Hovey and McCracken were among the dozens of companies that entered the field. As the industry developed, smaller operators inevitably were driven out of business. The survivors not only increasingly dominated the industry, but they also expanded their control over tens of thousands of acres of Arkansas's woodlands for current usage and for future development.

During the 1880s, mills to process timber sprang up at central locations near the forests with access to railroads. While the timber companies initially used small-scale, relatively portable mills for sawing timber, the larger companies invested more heavily in centralized, less mobile mills. To get the timber to these facilities, some companies became involved in railroading. The Gate City Lumber Company Railroad, chartered in 1886, brought wood from the forests to its plants in Texarkana and Shreveport, Louisiana. The Ultima Thule, Arkadelphia, and Mississippi, from Daleville to Ouachita in Dallas County, was originally chartered in 1877 and was owned by the Arkadelphia Lumber Company. Its primary use was to freight logs from the western part of Dallas County to the company's mills at Daleville. More commonly, the companies built hundreds of miles of temporary, usually narrow gauge, track into the forests to allow easier removal of the timber.

Major centers for processing emerged in the 1880s and 1890s. Sometimes these were located in larger communities, but more frequently they became the centers of towns whose very existence was owed to the mills—towns such as Waldo, Milner, Stamps, and Canfield. These mills usually took rough-cut lumber from country mills and planned and dressed it. Many of these plants were very large. In the 1890s Fordyce's Southern Land and Lumber Company boasted a mill capable of sawing 65,000 board feet of lumber and planing 75,000 feet while employing an average of two hundred men. At Lewisville, the Kansas-based Sunny South Lumber Company's plant, with a work force of one hundred fifty men, sawed 70,000 feet per day and had the capacity of planing 150,000 feet, and the locally owned Red River Lumber Company's one hundred fifty men cut some 70,000 to 80,000 feet per day. These mills represented an enormous investment of capital just in the facility itself.

The growth rate of the lumber and timber industry was rapid. In 1880 some 319 companies were engaged in the business and the value of their product was $1,793,848. Ten years later the total number of businesses had risen to 539 and their product to $8,943,052. In the 1890s, however, the industry's expansion was phenomenal. The number of establishments increased some 122 percent to 1,199 businesses. The value of the industry's product had grown at a rate of 168 percent to $23,959,983, making it the most important nonagricultural industry in the state financially. Lumber accounted for 64 percent of the value of manufactured goods produced in the state that year and 22 percent of the total value of the state's agricultural, mining, and manufactured goods.

For the majority of Arkansans, the most immediate benefit of the developing timber industry was the job opportunities created. Entrepreneurs used the local population as workers, since the industry required laborers with relatively few skills. Farm workers could make the transformation with ease, quickly moving into the forests were they harvested the timber or into the mills spreading throughout the state. When Ormond H. Twiford went to work in 1901 cutting logs at a camp at Cove, near Mena, he worked with a team that, using hand axes, usually cut down thirty to forty trees per day and trimmed them to haul to the mill. Twiford's wage was $1.75 per day for a six-day week, and a hay-filled bunk was provided by the company, though he had to pay $3.15 per week to eat at the nearby mill camp and time lost for whatever reason was subtracted from his pay. In fact, he actually only received about $12 for a month's work, below the census wage estimates of about ten cents per hour, or around $300 annually, in 1902 for loggers and men in the saw mills. Working conditions were not ideal and pay was not particularly good, but it was still better than the farm.

The railroads also expanded opportunities for the development of the state's mineral resources. By the late 1870s Arkansans were aware of a wide variety of potentially valuable mineral deposits across the state. Lead and zinc had been mined to some degree in the Ozarks. Silver deposits were believed to exist in the Ouachitas. A variety of bituminous coal existed in considerable quantity in western Arkansas and, associated with these fields and known to exist at this time, considerable pools of natural gas and oil. Other minerals that might be commercially mined also existed. Of all these, the coal fields were the first of the state's mineral resources to be developed, and by the turn of the century coal would be the most significant of the state's mining operations.

The opportunity to develop the coal fields of western Arkansas opened up primarily with the completion of the Fort Smith and Little Rock line in the 1870s. Mining activities were further encouraged after 1900 when the Choctaw, Oklahoma, and Gulf Railroad Company, which had purchased the Memphis and Little Rock, extended the latter's line into Oklahoma Territory. Mining ventures developed particularly in Sebastian, Johnson, and Pope Counties, with major mines operated at Jenny Lind, Huntington, Greenwood, Spadra, and Coal Hill.

In 1880 western mines had produced only 14,778 tons of coal. By 1890 production had increased to nearly 400,000 tons. At the turn of the century the companies mined nearly 2,000,000 tons. This yield had a sizable impact on the western counties, with a value of over $2.5 million. That represented, however, only a small portion of the total economic product of the state at the time. For the state at large, the boom in the coal industry brought about only a limited economic effect.

In addition to the value of the coal shipped out of Arkansas, the western mines also added to the economy as one of the largest single employers in the state. By 1902, 2,574 workers were employed in the fifty-three coal mines then in operation. Mine work, like labor in the timber industry, was hard. Nationwide, and probably in Arkansas in 1890, the average worker put in about fifty-two hours per week—five eight-hour days plus a half-day on Saturday. Work often was dangerous, usually uncomfortable. Laborers also had to compete with convict labor, leased from the state penitentiary, for their jobs. Still, relatively high wages made mining attractive. In 1902 Arkansas coal miners received over twenty-two cents per hour, an annual wage of $691 if the worker could remain fully employed. This was a considerable cash income at a time when money was hard to get on the farm.

Associated with the development of the coal fields, oil and gas were also commercially produced for the first time about the turn of the century. The first effort at commercial exploitation came in 1889, when Henry E. Kelley drilled an exploratory well in Scott County and discovered a small amount of both gas and oil. The well did not produce enough oil for commercial use; the gas, which was difficult to transport, was considered a nuisance and burned off. Nonetheless, the discovery encouraged further exploration. Through the 1890s, drillers sunk wells in unlikely locations such as Benton, Logan, and Conway Counties, but they never found the gusher they sought.

Ultimately, it was gas rather than oil that found a market first. Gas had some commercial uses, such as home heating and cooking. The lack of efficient means to get gas to potential consumers, however, meant that it had to be sold primarily in communities near the gas and oil fields. As a result, a limited demand developed in towns near the Mansfield and Massard Prairie pools of western Arkansas, and gas for business and home use was available at both Fort Smith and Van Buren. Like coal, oil and gas proved to be important economic activities where they were found, but for the state at large their development produced only limited economic improvement before the introduction of automobiles in the early twentieth century.

Mineral resources, long envisioned as one of the state's great attributes, were never really developed to the extent hoped for by the New South advocates in this early period. The size of deposits, demand, and the availability and cost of transportation combined to minimize effective commercial exploitation. In fact, except for coal, no other significant mining operations emerged in the first phase of New South economic transformation.

The development of a small manufacturing sector for the state's economy was the most important aspect of late-nineteenth-century economic growth, at least in terms of the value of goods produced. It offered Arkansans a real opportunity for prosperity, since entrepreneurs and labor would profit from their share of the money made from the value added to a product by the processing or fabrication of finished products from raw materials.

Arkansas industry emerged as a result of several major factors. Railroads and new technologies and fabrication techniques encouraged centralized processing of agricultural and timber products. Among the first industries to develop in railroad towns were those associated with a revolution taking place in ginning and compressing and those that attempted to manufacture finished wood products. In turn, these industries and the railroads themselves promoted the creation of other businesses that manufactured items that they needed—everything from saw mill machinery to railroad cars.

Industries related to cotton were the first to appear. Compressing and warehousing had always been an essential business associated with cotton production. A major problem in the marketing of cotton always centered around the cost of shipping. Compresses that existed earlier in the century were relatively inexpensive, but the bales they produced were large. In the 1880s steam compresses appeared that could reduce the size of the bale by one half, making shipment easier. These compresses, however, were more expensive and required a large investment of capital. Their advantages were such that compress activities shifted from the local gin to centralized facilities, and every community in Arkansas attempted to bring one to town.

The Pine Bluff Compress Company, formed in June 1884, was typical of the new operation. The company was actually organized by two Georgia businessmen in connection with a local cotton buyer. They issued capital stock valued at $50,000, a sizable amount at the time. Pressing 132 bales an hour and ultimately expanding its productivity to a capacity of 600 bales per day, the Pine Bluff Compress was a commercial success that quickly spawned competitors. In 1888 local citizens at Pine Bluff chartered the Standard Compress and Warehouse Company, capitalized at $200,000; the compress itself cost $32,000.

Through the 1880s and early 1890s, the industry experienced major changes. The major trend was toward a reduction in the number of compresses and the concentration of those that remained in the hands of fewer owners. By 1894, for example, Little Rock's Union Compress Company was one of the major companies in the state, operating two compresses at Little Rock, one at Newport, and another at Texarkana. As the machines became larger, securing a steady supply of cotton became more and more important, and this was accomplished usually by establishing broader ties with cotton brokers. In 1894 Union Compress sold $100,000 of its $350,000 in capital stock to the Lesser Cotton Company of St. Louis and to Paton, McClaren, and Company of Liverpool and New Orleans. Little Rock leaders saw an increase in business as the two companies, which purchased cotton from throughout the state, would send their cotton to Little Rock for compressing. Such actions was important in reducing the number of competing companies and concentrating power in the hands of a few major compresses.

Another significant new manufacturing activity to emerge during this period was the cottonseed-oil industry. The first mills in the state were introduced sometime in the 1870s, with Pine Bluff's Emma Oil Company, founded in 1875, and the Little Rock Oil and Compress, organized in 1877, among the first. These plants required considerable capitalization and, like the compress industry, as the century progressed they tended to be centrally located near railroad transportation. Little Rock Oil and Compress ultimately involved the investment of some $250,000 and became part of the New York–based Hurricane Cotton Oil Company. The Little Rock company's plant in North Little Rock was one of the largest in the South at the time of its construction in 1880, employed as many as 225 men, and processed 150 tons of cottonseed per day. The Arkansas Cotton Oil Company at Pine Bluff, opened in 1897, was valued at $100,000. Handling some 10,000 to 12,000 tons of seed per season, the mill could process 70 tons of seed per day. Even at Fort Smith, one of the largest industrial concerns in the city was the Fort Smith Oil and Cotton Compress Company, ginning from

10,000 to 12,000 bales of cotton per year and consuming some 10,000 tons of cottonseed each year.

The oil and processed seed had a ready market both domestically and overseas. The oil was used as a substitute for lard and olive oil and later became a major ingredient in margarine. The remaining seed was either pressed into cakes that were used as cattle feed or as fertilizer; in 1880 cake produced in Little Rock was shipped as far away as Great Britain. By 1890 officials of these companies spent millions of dollars buying what had previously been rubbish. By 1900 this industry was the second largest in the state in profitability.

The problem with the cottonseed industry was at first its seasonal nature. Full operations generally lasted from the beginning of October to the end of March each year. The railroads, however, made it possible for communities to expand their supplies of cottonseed by bringing it in from a more extensive geographic area. Mills in communities along railroads could therefore operate on a more consistent basis, though rate structures at times interfered with these efforts.

Compresses and oil mills were part of the industrial growth desired by Arkansans, but most developers saw the creation of cotton mills as the ultimate mark of economic progress. Transforming raw cotton into thread and textiles was a sophisticated industry and was believed to bring considerable economic advantage to the community. Arkansas's entrepreneurs actively tried to get mills located within the state, but they produced only modest results. The most common problem was that they were unable to secure enough capital from local investors to open mills, and outsiders generally stayed away from ventures not significantly backed by local interests. There were a few successes. The Arkansas Manufacturing Company at Arkadelphia consumed large quantities of cotton grown in southwestern Arkansas and manufactured it into cloth. Henry Merrill started this plant, which spun thread and carded wool, at Royston in Pike County in 1856. It was moved to Texas during the Civil War, then brought back to Royston, where it began to manufacture cloth. Moving to Arkadelphia in 1889, it continued to produce cloth through the century. Still, the company was one of the few that located in the state.

In addition to companies that processed the cotton crop, other industries developed that were tied to the state's grain crops. Large-scale milling and elevator operations became part of the new industrial mix after the 1880s. The railroads made possible the integration of larger producing and marketing regions and made it possible for corn and wheat to be brought to central locations for processing and storage. These new mills and facilities were much more expensive than the smaller operations of the recent past. The Pine Bluff Mill and Elevator Company was typical. Its elevators stored 75,000 bushels of grain, and its mills could roll some 200,000 pounds of grain daily. For its time, the mill represented a major investment of capital, costing $50,000 when built. Establishments like this one were aggressively and successfully recruited at Fort Smith and Little Rock.

The timber industry also produced efforts to manufacture more sophisticated goods in addition to the basic processing of logs into lumber; these companies themselves were usually major investors in such activities. Specialized mills prepared railroad ties, barrel staves, broom handles, and a variety of building materials such as shingles, window and door frames, and blinds. At Pine Bluff, the Bluff City Lumber Company was typical. Not only did it engage in extensive timber cutting through southern Arkansas, it also manufactured sashes, doors, and blinds, plus bank and bar fixtures.

Building materials such as these were the most common type of wood product manufactured locally, although some companies manufactured more intricate goods. The highly specialized Hardin Lumber Company at Fort Smith manufactured dressed and fancy lumber, scroll work, and cornice brackets. A few companies at Fort Smith and Little Rock attempted even more complicated work building furniture. By 1889 the Buddenberg Furniture Factory at Little Rock produced what was called a "common grade" of furniture marketed primarily in Arkansas. The Little Rock Chair Factory Company fabricated split, cane, and rattan bottom chairs that were sold throughout the Southwest.

As compresses and mills that processed cotton oil, textiles, grains, and wood products developed, they in turn encouraged the development of auxiliary industries. Little Rock reflected the interdependence of industrial activities. By 1890 the emergence of the city as a major compress and oil pressing center attracted other manufacturing concerns. Machine shops, such as the Union Machine Works and Foundry and the Little Rock Foundry and Machine Shops, provided essential services and goods. The latter specialized in repairing sawmill machinery and agricultural implements, but also manufactured boilers, engines, and architectural iron works. The Thomas Cotton Works manufactured the Thomas Cotton Press, producing over two hundred presses per year. The Eagle Cotton Ginnery and Pickory, in addition to regular ginning activity, bought up gin and oil mill refuse that was processed for companies that made paper stock, felt hats, and other such items. Little Rock Cooperage manufactured barrels primarily for cottonseed oil. The same interaction took place at Pine Bluff, where the Dilley Foundry Company, employing from fifty to sixty men, manufactured sawmill machinery, produced iron castings, and did general foundry work. It included among its major customers the St. Louis Southwestern, or Cotton Belt, Railway and its local shops. At Fort Smith, the Ketchum Iron Company manufactured steam engines, boilers, sawmills, sorghum mills, elevators, oil and gas well drilling equipment, and all kinds of architectural iron work, supplying the mechanical support for other businesses in the Fort Smith area.

The railroads also required supporting facilities and started their own operations that increased manufacturing and employment. The Cotton Belt constructed a major shop in Mechanicsville, an eastern suburb of Pine Bluff. These shops had the facilities to build all types of railroad equipment from cars, constructing most of the company's rolling stock, to engines. In addition to a simple expansion of employment, the railroads needed a variety of skilled workers, such as mechanics and engineers, to run the various aspects of the enterprise.

Ultimately, at least a few manufacturing concerns developed in Arkansas simply because entrepreneurs believed the state's central location along major transportation routes was ideally located to reach prospective markets. A correspondent of the *Gazette* in 1879 reported that Little Rock was becoming a center of manufacturing because of this advantage. Its shingle mills shipped their products to as far away as Texas. A cooperage factory sold its oil barrels and beer kegs in St. Louis. An ice plant filled orders as far out as Texarkana and Fort Smith. The correspondent optimistically concluded that Little Rock's economy would boom because it had an "immense scope of country which by well directed enterprise can be made tributary to it." Railroads made that trade possible, and at Little Rock and other central points along the roads, population expanded with the economic possibilities created.

The emergence of manufacturing represented a significant development in the state's overall economy. The numbers of industries and people involved in manufacturing did not represent a large part of the economic activity of the state, but the value of manufactured goods was substantial. Between 1880 and 1900, the value of manufactured goods increased from $6,756,159 to $45,197,731, some 569 percent. This compared well to the mere 82 percent growth of the value of agricultural products during the same period.

The significance of the changes taking place could be seen in the steady growth of the value of manufacturing establishments in the state compared with the value of farms. The latter increased approximately 60 percent during the 1880s, then 14 percent in the 1890s. The capital invested in manufacturing, however, increased at rates of 235 percent and 100 percent respectively during these same two decades. The value of capital invested in manufacturing as a part of the combined value of manufacturing capital and farm investment steadily climbed during this period. In 1880 manufacturing capital represented 4 percent of the total; ten years later it was 11 percent.

As in other industrial areas, higher-paying jobs were a major contribution of new business. Especially in manufacturing, the relative skills required meant that wages could be good. Overall, workers employed by manufacturers averaged only $327 per year in 1900, but that included everyone from timber cutters to day laborers. Workers with skills were more highly prized. That same year furniture makers averaged $396 and railroad shop employees $624. At the turn of the century, engineers and firemen on the Cotton Belt received a relatively high rate of pay at over $80 per month, boilermakers working for the Iron Mountain in North Little Rock made about $72, and mechanics at the Cotton Belt shops received approximately $60 per month. Wages in other industries were not as good, but employees of a brickyard at Little Rock received approximately 20 cents per hour in 1889, which gave them a monthly salary of $48, or an annual wage of $576. In the 1890s, foundry workers in Pine Bluff and Little Rock generally earned 17 cents per hour, or approximately $41 per month. Workers with the Arkansas Cotton Oil Company at Little Rock in 1897 brought home about 15 cents per hour, or $36 per month.

Overall, the new industries produced a major shift in the occupational structure of Arkansas labor. Between 1880 and 1900 there was a steady increase in the proportion of the total work force in the state whose work was connected with activities associated with the shift in marketing and transportation. The percentage of individuals employed in trade and transportation grew in these years from 3 percent of the total population to 7 percent. Those employed as mechanics or in manufacturing grew from 4 to 7 percent. Overall, the number of persons whose primary income was not from agriculture changed between 1880 and 1900 from 17 to 29 percent of the state's workers.

A final shift generated by the introduction of the railroads and the consequent restructuring of the state's economy was the encouragement that it gave to commerce, trade, and the many jobs associated with towns that grew and prospered as a result of the new economy. The railroads and the collapse of the antebellum factorage system moved the financing, marketing, and transporting of the state's crops as well as supplying the needs of the rural population from far-away centers to towns around the state, where local merchants financed both large and small farmers. Wolff-Goldman of Newport or McKenzie's General Store at Helena were typical, advancing credit to local farmers, offering dry goods, groceries, hardware, farm implements, and almost anything else a farmer could need, and also engaging in a wholesale trade with merchants in smaller towns or operating rural country stores. The new industries, centralized along the rail system, were primarily located in towns or cities. All this activity, in turn, generated new opportunities for those providing support to these urban people.

Economies of country villages and towns quickly grew in complexity. In 1889 Jonesboro had a population of only two thousand persons, but the town had a bank, six general stores, two groceries, eight drug stores, three dry good stores, and a clothing store. In addition, a variety of enterprises provided services to the expanding population. Five barbershops, twelve hotels, restaurants, boarding houses, and an undertaker made their living taking care of the needs of those businessmen engaged in the town's commercial activities. For larger towns such as Fort Smith, Helena, Little Rock, or Pine Bluff, the economic movement of the community was even greater with increasing business specialization.

Reflecting the growth of this economic sector was the steady increase in the number of workers involved. The proportion of workers employed in such activities increased from 4 to 7 percent between 1880 and 1890. Unfortunately, there is no way to measure the actual economic change that took place because of expanding business.

In time, the rise of urban economies produced an expansion of urban populations. For the people of the towns and cities, many of the values and ideas that had given meaning to life in the countryside no longer worked or made sense. Ultimately, built on an economic revolution, the towns and cities produced their own revolution, this one in basic social order. The transformation of society would be the real test of whether or not a "New Arkansas" could be created out of the "Old."

Urban Development

The economic changes that occurred in Arkansas after 1875 initiated a social revolution as well. In the 1880s and 1890s this social upheaval took place primarily in the villages, towns, and cities that boomed as a result of commercial and industrial prosperity. The town became the home of new peoples and a new society. They were also the place where a new culture emerged. All of these combined to help produce new ideas about social relationships that provided the roots for a transformation in government that would take place at the beginning of the twentieth century. Everything was changing, and for traditional Arkansas, the life of the town was as alien as that of any foreign country.

Towns were the chief beneficiaries of the new economy. They were the locations of many of the new jobs in manufacturing, in railroads, and in commerce. The most obvious results of this new economic opportunity was the expansion of old towns, the creation of new ones, and the steady urbanization of Arkansas's population. In 1880 only 4 percent of the people of the state were "urban," that is living in towns with 2,500 residents or more. By 1900 the urban population had reached 9 percent. The three largest towns at the turn of the century had all tripled in size from 1880—Little Rock from 13,138 to 38,307; Fort Smith from 3,099 to 11,587; and Pine Bluff from 3,203 to 11,492.

The move to the city did not affect the older and larger towns alone, however. Villages such as Arkadelphia, Camden, Eureka Springs, Fayetteville, Jonesboro, Mena, Newport, Paragould, Texarkana, and Van Buren, among others, reached urban status between 1880 and 1900. Railroad and local marketing centers also experienced remarkable growth. Fordyce, created by the Cotton Belt in 1883 to provide shipping facilities for products from Dallas, Calhoun, and Cleveland Counties, was typical. That town grew from vacant lots when the railroad reached it to 1,710 inhabitants by the turn of the century. Others were just as successful.

The expansion of the towns was more than a simple demographic shift. It also represented a social revolution that refashioned the lives of the rural Arkansans who moved to town. People moved from communities with relatively homogeneous populations to ones with remarkable diversity among their peoples. Towns had always been more heterogeneous than the countryside in their populations, but this character was strengthened by new growth. Urban society was marked by greater differences in ethnicity and regional origins, a more complex system of class, and modification of the racial order.

The majority of white and black urban citizens remained Southern-born in this period, just like in the countryside, but towns were filled with increased numbers of people from various backgrounds. Ethnic diversity was one of the features of the more heterogeneous population. Little Rock traditionally had a larger number of foreign-born citizens, but by 1900 these foreigners represented 5 percent of the city's population, compared with less than 1 percent for the whole state. Fort Smith and Hot Springs had foreign-born communities that represented about the same proportion of their populations as well.

The origins of Little Rock's foreign-born people probably reflected the pattern found in other towns. Over half of the immigrants were from Central Europe, particularly Germany. The Irish were the second largest ethnic community in the capital. Other groups were statistically less important, but they were significant for the diversity that they brought to the city. At the turn of the century, Little Rock's foreign-born population included Chinese, Greeks, Italians, Mexicans, Poles, Russians, and even Turks.

At least during the lives of the first generation of immigrants, the foreigners often retained parts of their ethnic heritage and thus added to the unique character of life in the urban setting. Many Germans in Little Rock settled in their own neighborhood around St. Edward's Catholic Church and maintained German social and political organizations plus a

German language newspaper, the *Arkansas Staats Zeitung*. In the early 1890s the Little Rock community held "German Days" in early October, something like the German Oktoberfest, that was attended by Arkansans of German origin from throughout the state. The Irish never established their own neighborhoods in Little Rock, but they did introduce a few institutions such as the Sons of Erin, a social club that allowed them to retain contact with each other and their native culture.

Arkansas's towns were not just home to larger numbers of foreigners, however. They also contained significant numbers of Northerners who had come to the state following the Civil War. A few of them might be considered "Carpetbaggers," a derogatory term applied to those who came south at the end of the Civil War to secure political advantages. The majority, however, were individuals who came to what they considered an economic frontier, moving as Americans had done for generations to new areas where they hoped to make their fortune. The development of new industries offered such opportunities, and Northerners were well-represented among the managers and white-collar workers of these new enterprises.

Like the foreign-born, the Northern immigrants to Arkansas's towns brought a culture that contrasted with that of the people around them. The most noteworthy aspect of their differences were those created by the Civil War. Some of these men had served in the Union army during the Civil War, and they sponsored organizations such as the Grand Army of the Republic and the Loyal Legion, two Union army veterans groups. Politically, many of them were Republicans, often retaining ties with Republican politicians from their home states.

In addition to the diverse national and regional backgrounds of the inhabitants, changes in social relationships added to the complexity of town life. Among whites, new classes came into existence as a result of the economic changes taking place. Towns had always possessed an elite of successful businessmen and craftsmen, as well as a class of entrepreneurs less successful or just starting out. Unskilled laborers and day laborers had always existed as a lower economic group, although many of them lived in a town for only a short time until they moved on either to the countryside or to another city. These classes were now joined by new ones produced by the economic revolution in late-nineteenth-century Arkansas.

For the urban business class, the new economy produced few changes in social position. Proportional to the general population its size was reduced, but its wealth increased. By 1900, for example, slightly more than 7 percent of the people in Little Rock were part of the entrepreneurial class of bankers, brokers, wholesalers, and retailers. Compared with earlier years, their wealth apparently had increased. At Little Rock and in every other town, the homes of the merchants indicated a prosperity beyond anything achieved earlier in the century. Streets lined with Victorian mansions showed the owners' economic power to build and furnish monuments to success.

The lower class of unskilled workers also remained largely unchanged from that of earlier years, although increasing in size with the expansion of opportunities for the kinds of work they could perform. Constituting about 17 percent of the white work force at Little Rock, this under class remained at the bottom. Their wages were modest, probably not much better than what they could receive on farms. The chances of getting ahead, as always, were small. Most workers lived from day to day, hoping that an illness would not prevent them from working or that their employer had not laid them off as they reported to work each morning.

The status of the businessman, however, was challenged by the emergence of a new middle class. This class was not simply "in the middle," it represented a new group whose position in society was based on the knowledge and skills they possessed. These individuals did not own a business but worked for others. Their particular expertise, however, made them essential to the community's life. In Little Rock by 1900, about 17 percent of the work force filled jobs that made them part of the developing middle class, working as professionals such as teachers, attorneys, physicians, dentists, clergymen, architects, electricians, managers, and engineers. Also included were white-collar workers essential to the operations of the new businesses —bookkeepers and accountants, clerks, copyists, stenographers, "typewriters," and telegraph workers.

The income of the professionals is impossible to estimate. The census, however, provided information on the salaries of white-collar workers, and they generally earned almost 35 percent more than the highest-paid skilled workers. The income of the professionals would likely have been at least another 35 percent higher than white-collar workers. For both groups, the relative prosperity was evidenced, just as with the business class, by the material possessions with which they surrounded themselves.

The clearest distinction separating the middle class from the traditional business class and rural peoples, however, was the set of values to which it adhered. The class's success was tied to its mastery of formal and often technical knowledge essential to the new economy and society. With their position so closely linked to education, it was logical for these people to view formal education as a critical goal for their children and even society, to regard knowledge based upon "scientific" analysis as the key to progress. The ultimate triumph of these ideas for society in general added greatly to the importance and power of this class in subsequent years.

The new middle class was not the only group to appear in the urban environment of New South Arkansas. In addition, the railroads and factories also attracted a new class of skilled workers. There had always been such individuals in Arkansas towns, but they usually owned their own businesses. These laborers, however, worked for wages high enough to give them considerable earning power. Those in this class—railroad workers and some skilled factory employees such as engineers, machinists, and boiler makers, plus skilled craftsmen in various trades—constituted roughly 59 percent of the work force in Little Rock at the turn of the century. In Pine Bluff, with large railroad shops, the percentage may have been even greater.

This large portion of urban society has had little written about it and its character is less known than perhaps any other social group in Arkansas. A program for a Pine Bluff fair in 1897 provides some insight into this class, most of whom worked in the St. Louis Southwestern's main shops. Their wages were good and added to the town's prosperity, but the writer was also impressed with their civic virtues. They usually owned their own homes. Their children were in schools. They demonstrated, in this manner, many of the same values that were apparent in the middle class, which suggests they probably envisioned their own futures as tied closely to middle class ideas.

The new urban society was much more complex than that found in the countryside, but this complexity was nowhere greater and the challenge to the status quo of more importance than in matters of race. By definition, African-Americans constituted a permanent under class in rural society, and the economic position of the majority of them ensured that this was not challenged. In the towns, however, African-Americans were still considered to be inferiors, but the demand for labor and the unique circumstances of urban life allowed at least some to achieve economic success of a magnitude that challenged normal racial standards.

The emergence of a relatively prosperous African-American community in Arkansas's towns was rooted in the success of black laborers who secured jobs in the new mills and the railroads and those who provided services for the expanding white business and middle classes. In Little Rock in 1894, roughly 14 percent of all black workers were employed by railroads or mills. Most of these were common laborers, but at least a few were blacksmiths and machinists. Another 11 percent were the women who worked as domestic servants and laundresses for the white community. Often paid less than their white counterparts, they still received a wage that made them much better off than the African-American farmers, and they also provided a base of consumers for the services of black entrepreneurs and professionals.

The black elite presented a major challenge to the racial status quo. Particularly in Helena, Little Rock, and Pine Bluff, prosperous black entrepreneurs emerged. By 1900 a business directory at Pine Bluff listed some 235 black businessmen. Although a few of them had a white trade, the majority provided services for African-Americans. They worked as barbers, confectioners, grocers, hotelier, saloonkeepers, restauranteurs, and in almost any other type of business enterprise. Wiley Jones of Pine Bluff proved one of the more successful: starting with a mercantile store, he expanded his operations to a saloon, then purchased town lots, race horses, and even one of the town's streetcar lines.

These businessmen were joined in their prosperity by a small group of professionals. By the turn of the century, physicians such as D. B. Gaines, a graduate of Nashville's Meharry Medical College, and others practiced medicine at Little Rock. Scipio A. Jones was dean of African-American attorneys in the capital city and licensed to practice before the United States Supreme Court. Mifflin W. Gibbs, another Little Rock lawyer, not only practiced law but also had become part of the business elite as president of Capital City Savings Bank, one of the only African-American financial institutions in the city.

These African-Americans presented real threats to accepted definitions of racial position. Their wealth made it possible for them to live a lifestyle similar to their white counterparts, and it also raised ambitions among them for even more. African-American farm workers presented few problems to white society, for they seldom had any opportunities to move in the white world. Prosperous middle-class African-Americans, however, had the money to ride trains, to stay in hotels, to eat in restaurants, or to attend the theater. Convention insisted that the races be separated, but economic forces no longer ensured that would happen.

While society was becoming more intricate with the development of new institutions, the nature of the most important of all of these institutions in rural communities, the family, was rapidly acquiring a new form with new roles. This new urban family remained an important institution, but it lost many of its traditional functions. The most profound difference between the urban family and its rural counterpart was that it no longer had the same economic cohesion, with all of its members working to produce a livelihood. In the urban environment, the workplace was not connected with the family in the same way that it had been on the farm. Wage earners left their homes early each morning and usually did not return until the end of their ten-hour day. While the new work was more profitable than that of the farm, the worker could no longer easily perform other tasks associated with family life.

Attempting to carry out all of the various functions of a family, its members specialized their activities. One member, usually the father, became the primary wage earner, responsible for the family's economic survival. At least in theory, the urban family remained a patriarchy, dominated by the father, but the father's role in day-to-day life was necessarily curtailed. On the job through most of every day, fathers no longer had the opportunities to engage in tasks in which they traditional participated, including education and socialization of the children.

Wives' work remained associated with the household, just like the women of the countryside, but now it was her exclusive place of labor, and the nature of that work was changing. To begin with, wives no longer contributed directly to the family's wealth by producing goods that could be sold. Furthermore, even the manufacture of household goods declined as items such as soap and clothing became readily available at inexpensive prices in stores. Accessibility to prepared foods even helped to revolutionize food preparation, although gardening, slaughtering, and cooking still remained an important part of household work. The mother of Boyce House, a druggist's son from Brinkley, still cooked and did daily cleaning chores while House was a youth, but her husband's good income allowed her to bring a maid to their home once or twice a week to help with heavier jobs and to wash and iron the clothes. The end result of this transformation of household work was to provide urban women with greater freedom for other pursuits.

In the framework of the changing activities connected with the household, ideas about a woman's position within the family (beyond mother to children) and the community became less clear. Some thought that women should remain primarily within the household, although she would spend more of her time devoted to raising the children (in the absence of the father) or to adding to the beauty and comfort of their homes. The good housewife took steps to make sure that her home was in the best taste, her children were well-behaved, and that she herself was an object of pride to her husband. Articles appearing in new national magazines such as *Ladies Home Journal, Woman's Home Companion,* and *McCall's* (and on the "Women's Page" of the Sunday newspapers) guided a woman in carrying out her role with advice on how to clean walls, redecorate a house, make salads, be fashionable and beautiful by using "Mme. M. Yale's Beauty Secrets" or "Harriet Hubbar Ayer's Recamier Toilet Preparations," or most importantly, model her home and her life along the same lines as "refined" women.

This new role, with a woman's total subordination to domestic affairs, represented one model of change in the urban world, but it was not the only one that emerged. Freedom from some of the traditional work of the household also undermined rigid definitions of gender roles. Some women considered whether or not their peculiar female attributes might allow them to play a larger role in society. As early as the mid-1880s, Mary W. Loughborough, publisher of the *Arkansas Ladies' Journal,* asked if woman's unique nature could not produce good in the public arena and pondered how this might be done.

Many women concluded that they did have a larger role to play. The women's clubs that appeared in towns across the state in the 1880s and 1890s became the principal vehicles for action. Little Rock's Aesthetic and the Edelweiss Clubs, the Searcy Social Club, the Osceola Pansy Book Club, the Bald Knob Sunshine Club, and twenty-four other organizations were all part of a state movement that united into the Arkansas Federation of Women's Clubs in 1898. The focus of each individual club was different, but most of them were interested in some sort of activism as well as providing a social function for their members. Meetings had entertainment, but they also usually included a serious presentation dealing with contemporary social problems and their solutions. Typical programs in 1898 included lectures on "Modern Education—Is It Modern?" "Education as a Preventive of Crime," "America—Her Part in History and Her Destiny," "The Club Woman," and "Women as Patriots." The first state convention considered a variety of educational issues, including child study, traveling libraries, aids to self-education, industrial and reform schools, and what women could do for public education.

At least in the beginning, few of the club members concluded that a greater role in the community would lead to women's suffrage, although for some that conclusion was part of an inevitable logic. This was true in particular for those who joined the Arkansas Woman's Christian Temperance Union, organized in 1879 to promote temperance in the use of alcohol. They began to play a role in politics in 1881, when the legislature allowed women to vote on local liquor licensing. By 1884 many women had become active in such local elections, and others played an increasing role in trying to push the state's Democratic and Republican Parties to adopt temperance planks in their platforms.

Ultimately, some women's groups moved on to demand full participation in the political process in order to further their agendas of reform. The first women's suffrage organization in the state was formed at Eureka Springs in 1884, but the Little Rock Equal Suffrage Association, organized by Clara A. McDiarmid in 1888, more directly influenced the future movement. The Arkansas Equal Suffrage Association emerged from the Little Rock group in 1893. McDiarmid, an attorney in Kansas before she moved to Arkansas, determined to fight for the vote when she discovered that rights she had held in Kansas did not exist in her new home. Initially, the Equal Suffrage Association did not attract widespread support among women, and McDiarmid's death in 1899 was a major setback. As women became increasingly active in community affairs, however, pressure grew to include them in the political process. While progress was slow, support emerged during the Progressive reform movement of the early twentieth century that secured the vote for women.

The circumstances of children also changed in the new setting. For the urban family, a child's labor was either no longer necessary or no longer appropriate. Urban prosperity made it unnecessary for some children to work. For those less fortunate, the nature of work in the urban economy made finding jobs more difficult. Farm children might work alongside of their fathers and mothers in the fields, but in the town they would have to enter the work force as an adult and alone. Although economic necessity forced some children to do exactly this, most did not.

With children either not having to work or unable to enter the work force, their lives changed considerably. More time could be devoted to a prolonged childhood in which the carefree years of play and irresponsibility were extended. For the more fortunate, this lengthening of childhood might even extend through college years and into the individual's early twenties. As in the case of parents, a new role for children required definition and instruction. This need provided the basis for a whole new literature that focused on the needs of children. Magazines such as the *Youth's Companion,* five-cent weeklies with stories about Buffalo Bill, Nick Carter, Frank

Merriwell, or Horatio Alger provided children with entertainment, suggestions for activities, and a sprinkling of education about morality and behavior suitable to their place.

The changes in family roles reflected the demands of the new society around it, and these new families appeared to be economically stronger. There were social costs connected with the change, however. For men, the participation in the day-to-day life of the family became limited. This did not mean that fathers were more or less affectionate and caring than those in farm families. It did mean that they simply had less direct input into family life. Wives, as a result of the new conditions, had a less certain place. Those who chose to become the "new housewife" paid the price of centering much of their lives on their children, with lessening attachment to the world of their husbands. Children lost their fathers as direct role models and from their mothers could learn little other than household management. The family no longer served to teach children how to survive in the new economy.

As would be expected, with institutions as basic as family, class, and race in transition, urban culture would be changing as well. In towns, new institutions vied with old as the mechanisms through which a community's ideas and values developed, and these were transmitted to their members. Among the major transitions taking place was the role of religion in the urban world. From standing almost alone as the arbiter of values, churches now were forced to compete with others for that role in the new communities.

The power of churches to define and enforce clear values in the larger town was reduced, if for no other reason, by the diversity of religious life that existed there. The heterogeneity of the population brought with it a mixed religious scene. While in the state's rural areas over 78 percent of churchgoers were Baptists or members of the Methodist Episcopal Church, South, these two denominations combined accounted for only 35 percent of churchgoers in Little Rock in 1900. City residents found many other Protestant churches to attend. Presbyterians, another large rural denomination, were present. The Methodist Episcopal Church, usually perceived as a northern church from which the Methodist Episcopal Church, South, had separated before the Civil War, had a congregation. Lutherans, almost nonexistent in the countryside, established themselves in the city. Additionally, Adventists, Church of Christ Scientist, Independents, Salvationists, Spiritualists, and Universalists held services at Little Rock. Other towns had an equally diverse Protestant community.

The clearest indicator of the deviation of urban religious life from that of the countryside, however, was the fact that the largest single urban denomination in 1900 was not even Protestant, it was Roman Catholic. In Little Rock in that year, over 23 percent of the citizens who stated a religious preference claimed to be Catholic. New residents, both from the rest of the nation and overseas, added to the strength of Catholic churches making it possible for the denomination to establish a formidable presence with educational and charitable institutions. At Little Rock, German Catholics built St. Edward's School for their children and the Sisters of Mercy operated St. Mary's Academy for girls and St. Joseph's for boys. At Helena, Catholics ran the Academy of the Sacred Heart and in Pine Bluff their schools included St. Joseph's and an industrial school for African-Americans. The church also backed Little Rock's Charity Hospital, established in 1887, and St. John's Hospital in Fort Smith.

Adding to religious diversity, the towns and cities also were the home of most of the state's Jewish people. Many Arkansas Jews were German in origin, migrating to the state primarily after the Civil War. In 1866 new settlers organized Pine Bluff's Congregation Anshe Emeth, and in 1870 Little Rock's Jews formed Congregation B'Nai Israel. These congregations were active in their communities. At Little Rock, the rabbi's sermons were usually included in the weekly newspaper reports of church activities along with those of his Christian counterparts.

The large number of churches indicated that people of the towns were religious, but variety prohibited the development of a common identity or set of values. Instead of speaking with a single voice, as was possible in the rural neighborhoods where everyone attended a single church, the diversity of religion undermined the ability of the community to approach problems with unity. There was a much greater freedom of belief and expression as a result, but the cost was the clarity of religious views that typified the rural congregation and, subsequently, the rural community.

Few issues pointed up the breakdown of cultural consensus in religious matters more than debates in the 1880s over Sunday closing laws. State and city restrictions on which business activities and entertainments could be carried out on the Christian Sabbath had existed in the antebellum years. Prohibited were the sale of most store goods as well as gambling, horse racing, and the sale of liquor. Through the 1870s, however, questions increased as to exactly what activities were prohibited by the law, with the occasional arrest of children who had gone fishing pointing up the ambiguities in the law and the unevenness of its enforcement. As towns grew, questions increased as did avoidance of the law. Opponents, such as Jews and Seventh Day Advents who observed the Sabbath on Saturdays, argued that such laws interfered with their freedom. Some citizens, unable to shop and do business during weekdays because of work, demanded that necessary businesses be allowed to stay open.

By 1878 church leaders in Little Rock expressed serious concern that the Sabbath was being desecrated by those who carried out business transactions and by "pleasure seekers." The breakdown of consensus on the enforcement of the law led to the creation of a society to enforce the Sabbath in 1882 and to extensive debates over the concept thereafter. In 1887 the Pastors Association in Little Rock condemned not only Sunday work but also entertainments, going so far as to denounce reading Sunday newspapers. When the nationally famous Gilmore Band appeared at Little Rock on a Sunday in 1888, it attracted a large crowd but spurred a lengthy debate among the town's ministers about the propriety of the performance. Ministerial influence ultimately caused town and state governments to ban a variety of activities, including playing baseball, but the consensus was difficult to maintain.

The integration of towns and cities into a wider national community through railroads and new communication systems intensified the diversity of ideas that broke down the homogeneous world of rural folks. Railroads not only made travel easier, but inexpensive mail deliveries accelerated the dissemination of information. The introduction of the telegraph and telephone may have been even more revolutionary in their affect on town culture. By the 1870s the Western Union Telegraph Company had tied Little Rock to the rest of the nation with telegraph service. In 1879 the same company opened the first telephone exchange at Little Rock, only two years after Alexander Graham Bell's invention appeared, and during the 1880s and 1890s telephone systems expanded their long-distance service, linking towns throughout Arkansas.

The result of new information systems was a flood of knowledge and ideas. Inexpensive national magazines such as *Harper's, Atlantic,* and *Scribner's Monthly* let the Arkansan know what was current in everything from literature to public issues. Associated Press reports, provided daily to the *Arkansas Gazette* after 1880, informed people about events throughout the nation almost immediately. Traveling shows brought New York productions to even the smallest town along the railroads. Subscribers to the 1893 Little Rock Lyceum Association's winter series could hear English bell ringers, a humorist talk about the "Rise and Fall of the Mustache," William H. "Coin" Harvey talk about the economy, or Gen. John B. Gordon, a former Confederate officer, lecture on "How Long will the Republic Live?" The urban resident was overwhelmed with facts and opinions in such a milieu.

The public was forced to assimilate the complexities of the urban world. Traditional ideas about the social order were being challenged by new conditions. Critical institutions no longer worked the way they had in the countryside. Families transmitted social information and work skills appropriate to the farm, but they did not necessarily provide the intellectual skills and the technological knowledge necessary in the new society. Religion only added to the dissonance confronted by the urban Arkansan. Within this disordered social framework, public schools, as well as ideas about the nature and role of formal education, emerged as the central institutions of the new urban social life.

A state-funded public school system had not been created in Arkansas until Reconstruction. Organized with the purposes of securing social order and economic progress, this first system was highly centralized and supported by state taxes. The Redeemers reorganized education after 1874 by placing control and primary financing of schools in the hands of local districts, with the result that the number of both schools and districts expanded throughout the rest of the century. Towns were particularly active in encouraging public education. Viewing this as essential to the well being of their communities, townspeople levied and paid the taxes necessary to create schools more willingly than rural Arkansans.

More significant than the expansion of the numbers of schools, however, was a change in the basic function of these institutions. Even in the private schools and those few public institutions that existed prior to the development of the postwar state system, the curriculum generally consisted of courses in basic reading, writing, and arithmetic. Beyond that, they offered subjects that imparted information considered to be the mark of the "educated" person. Increasingly, however, the schools shifted from teaching information to instruction that emphasized how to learn.

The shift in community need and in the role of education was mirrored particularly in the ideas of teachers themselves. In annual meetings of the Arkansas Teachers' Association, participants advanced the idea that being educated entailed more than simply learning information: schools had to teach their students how to think. J. W. Conger of Searcy put the point clearly in a speech that he made to the Arkansas Teachers Association in 1884 when he observed that in education, it was not "the number or importance of facts, but the use of them, which performs the ultimate results." Schools were to provide their students with the resources necessary to observe, gather facts, and develop their own answers to the problems they faced. Based upon the scientific ideas of knowledge, this approach contained the revolutionary assumption that truth was not fixed but simply sets of propositions, derived from observation and analysis, that explained phenomena. It was a system that allowed individuals to cope with a world where traditional ideas no longer explained realities.

Ideas about government and its role in society was another area in which the urban setting brought about major changes. By the end of the nineteenth century, local, county, and state governments had seen their basic roles widely expanded. Local authorities were expected to provide many basic services for their communities or to direct and supervise private enterprises that did. Local and state governments were also expected to define more clearly a variety of relationships within the community. The end result in every case was that urban government was more active than its rural counterpart.

The expansion of the functions of local government closely paralleled national trends at this time. In the town setting, many tasks the rural citizen would have taken care of personally now required community action. In addition to public education, urban residents increasingly considered more simple needs, such as securing safe drinking water, waste disposal, protection from fire, public safety, and transportation as community responsibilities. Usually through a combination of government and private effort, municipal or commercial enterprises were organized to meet these needs.

The difficulties created by Little Rock's growth pushed that city to take the lead in the expansion of services. Health problems forced officials in the late 1870s to reexamine the city's practice of obtaining water directly from the Arkansas River. Health concerns also suggested that the dumping of waste and sewage into a small creek known as Town Branch was detrimental to public safety. Rising fire insurance premiums caused by costly losses pointed out the inadequacies of volunteer fire companies. The presence of crime showed the failure of existing police measures. The impassability of streets in rainy weather and the spread of the town's boundaries created noticeable transportation problems.

Forced to respond, Little Rock created government agencies or supported private businesses that offered solutions. The answers were similar to those of cities elsewhere in the nation, and other communities within the state followed the same model. In 1877 the Little Rock Water Works developed wells to supply water and laid water mains throughout the city, ultimately installing a filtration system in 1891. The following year the city put in pipes for a sewage system. The town's professional police force, developed during Reconstruction, was expanded in these years. In 1892 the city formed its first professional fire department. Street paving and the introduction of street cars, mule-drawn in the 1870s and electric after the Little Rock Electric Street Railway Company was chartered in 1887, solved the town's transportation problems. Even if the government did not provide all of these services itself, the city now had the responsibility to make sure that they existed.

The increasing activity of government ran far beyond the provision of basic services or regulating utilities. In this era, government also engaged in the regulation of social relations. As traditional class and race lines blurred in urban society, people turned to government to define more clearly proper relations and behaviors. Citizens expected city officials to provide standards against which individuals could be measured and differences discerned.

The use of government to define and protect professions was the clearest class legislation of the era. In a world where personal acquaintance with individuals who provided services was no longer possible, some system was necessary to protect the consumer and ensure the quality of providers. The development of professions helped establish such standards. At the same time, professional organizations actually helped to create and maintain special privileges for their members. Government was central to that effort.

Physicians formed the first modern professional associations in Arkansas, following the lead of their contemporaries elsewhere in the nation. Historically, the treatment of diseases had been considered something of an art. Rival disease theories contended for acceptance, and self-proclaimed doctors offered cures for every known ailment. Those who believed that they had legitimate medicines vied with outright frauds for public support. This situation changed as the development of the germ theory and medical statistics created a scientific basis for medicine and gave physicians both an avenue into the treatment of disease and a measure of their effectiveness.

In 1870 physicians who had embraced this "new" medicine organized the State Medical Society of Arkansas. Throughout its early history, the society strove for government regulation of medical practice. Its goal of standardizing medical practice on scientific principles was an attempt to protect the public from nonprofessionals who made false claims about their particular practice and medicines. Dr. Daniel A. Linthicum of Helena, president of the organization in 1873, saw regulation as necessary to protect the people of the state from "charlatans and montebanks." While the motives of the medical society were an improvement in medical class, it was clear as well that the measures they pushed worked to limit medical competition by restricting access to practice. Government, as a result, not only controlled medicine, it also ensured the social status of physicians through regulation.

The obvious success of the new scientific medicine gave its practitioners considerable power in the state legislature, where they were successful in having implemented many of their goals. Physicians obtained a licensing law in 1881 that allowed county medical boards to determine the competency of candidates to practice medicine and to grant licenses. That was not enough, however, and through the pages of the *Journal of the State Medical Society*, members pushed to further regulate licensing. The society accomplished a major goal in 1903 when the legislature created state examining boards to administer prospective physicians, homeopaths, and eclectic practitioners. A bill in 1909 required candidates for medical licensing to have graduated from established medical schools and even helped define curricula by requiring applicants to be examined in specific medical areas. Licensing, standardization of practice, and a specific curriculum established the foundation of the profession.

The success of physicians in defining an accepted body of knowledge necessary to practice medicine and in gaining control over who could practice provided a model that many others sought to mimic. Pharmacists created the Arkansas Association of Pharmacists in 1883. They immediately sought government control over those who could engage in the sale or manufacture of drugs, which was realized in 1891 with the creation of a state board of pharmacy. Dentists organized their association in 1887, securing licensing laws in 1901.

In areas where standards for pursuing an occupation were not as easily determined, professionalization was difficult, but progress was made anyway. Central to the effort was the creation of professional associations. Lawyers began their move with the organization of the state bar association in 1882 to advance the "science" of jurisprudence and to "uphold the honor" of the profession. In 1887 engineers and others created the Arkansas Society of Engineers, Architects, and Surveyors. School teachers, through the Arkansas Teachers Association, pushed for the formation of schools of education, a curriculum for educating and training teachers, and licensing.

Groups as varied as the State Association of Fire Underwriters, the Retail Grocers' and Merchant's Association, and even the Arkansas Sheriff's Association worked to establish professional standards for their jobs, to fulfill what historian Robert Wiebe has called a "Search for Order."

As with the medical professions, these groups sought to establish even greater control by requiring the possession of a state license to practice in Arkansas. Continuing the use of government to protect their position, embalmers secured legislation establishing a state licensing board in 1909. In 1911 the assembly established licensing requirements for teachers and plumbers. Veterinarians followed in 1915. Lawyers, already subjected to local board examinations, were required to pass a state board exam after 1917. All of these groups had established professional associations, had worked to set the criterion for practice in their professions, and then secured firm control through legislative action. In doing this, they standardized their work, but they also limited competition by restricting entry into their professions.

In issues of race, where simple violence as practiced in the countryside could no longer hold the color line, government also played an increasingly active role as it undertook the task of maintaining racial separation. Actions in many different areas reinforced the basic racial divisions of society. The struggle over educational curricula at the state's Branch Normal College, later the University of Arkansas at Pine Bluff, and in the public schools for blacks reflected the tensions generated by the progress of African-Americans. Branch Normal, created in 1873 and offering high school and college courses for blacks, had always offered a classical curriculum. Principal Joseph C. Corbin and the school's teachers believed that African-American scholars should receive the same education as provided in the white schools of the state, and they, in turn, influenced the teachers they prepared.

During the 1880s, however, many white politicians began to urge that the curriculum abandon its traditional offerings in favor of training in practical skills. The question divided even the African-American community and reflected a similar national debate. The whole idea of offering education in farming and the trades had been advanced by Booker T. Washington of Tuskegee Institute in Alabama, and this philosophy was supported locally by prominent black leaders such as John E. Bush and Mifflin W. Gibbs. Washington's opponents did not oppose the value of agricultural and technical training as much as the implied neglect of classical education, which was still considered essential for entry into professions. National men like William E. B. Du Bois, Harvard's first black Ph.D. and a professor at

Atlanta University, and local leaders such as Corbin opposed any abandonment of classical education.

Ultimately, however, the advocates for limiting black education to industrial training triumphed at Branch Normal and in the public schools. White members of Branch Normal's board secured the appointment of Isaac Fisher to replace Corbin as principal in 1902. Fisher, who was a student of Washington at Tuskegee, brought that school's curriculum to Arkansas, greatly expanding industrial education. Some students and members of the community resisted Fisher's efforts, and he was never completely successful, but the changes were serious enough that African-Americans seeking access to the professions were forced to look out of state for their education. In changing curricula, whites limited opportunities for blacks and established sharper definitions of racial differences.

More to the point in establishing a clear color line between whites and blacks were legislative efforts during the 1890s to segregate public facilities. Middle class African-Americans posed a problem as they achieved an economic position that would have allowed them greater access to traditionally segregated privileges. On the railroads, blacks and whites had always ridden together in the coaches; economics had kept blacks out of the first-class accommodations. Prosperity changed that, and members of the black elites sought any accommodations they could afford. By 1885 white newspapers were demanding that the railroads run separate cars for blacks, but they found resistance not only from African-Americans but also from the railroads, which viewed separate facilities as too expensive.

White leaders who took up the segregationist cause responded with a vicious attack on blacks as a race, arguing in newspapers and elsewhere that blacks were unclean and behaved in ways that made their company with whites undesirable. Lumping together field hands and the black middle class, segregationists demanded that all blacks be prevented from securing access to white facilities. By 1890 the problem had become a major political issue, with the Democratic Party and Gov. James P. Eagle urging passage of a "Separate Coach Law." Although blacks opposed such legislation, it easily passed the general assembly in February 1891, the first of numerous laws that legally secured separation between the races and restored "order" to a social world in turmoil.

Public services, professional licensing, segregation—all of these activities and measures helped change the nature of government in Arkansas. Pressure toward greater activism increased in response to the turmoil created by problems on the farm in the 1880s and 1890s and would further the revolution in government.

For many contemporaries, the cities appeared to be the future of Arkansas: Their economies flourished. Their cultures appeared to be rich and varied when compared to that of the countryside. They were at the heart of change and seemed to reflect the inevitable end of progress. Their people exercised an increasingly powerful role in the life of the state as a whole. What was taking place in the towns, however, could not hide deteriorating conditions in the countryside. Through the 1880s and into the 1890s, already bad conditions on the farm worsened and gave rise to considerable social upheaval.

Families

James, Edwin, Mary, and Louise Reid were members of a prosperous Little Rock family, typical of the townspeople of the New South. James was a banker who had wed Mary Parker in 1892 and formed a partnership with her father. Mary took over the business, Parker, Reid, and Company, when James died in 1908, followed by the death of her father. She sold the company to Union Trust in 1910.

Hattie Hines Gillespie, shown with her husband, Ross, and children in 1915, was a teacher in Little Rock. She formed a part of the growing black professional class in Arkansas's towns.

George Lehman Hines Collection,
Arkansas History Commission, Little Rock

*William F. Burton, surrounded by
his family, was thirty-eight years
old when this picture was made in
1908. Burton farmed in Saline
County and owned his own land,
although like other Arkansas farms,
it had been mortgaged. He is
shown here with his wife, Clarice,
aged thirty-three, and his daughters
Cledia, eleven; Sarah, nine;
Theadine, two; and his recently-
born twins, Treecy and Tyriza.*

Arkansas History Commission,
Little Rock

Elisha Whitfield and his family were photographed on the porch of their home in Saline County about 1910. He was a tenant farmer who did not own the land he worked. Some tenants rented for cash rather than crop shares, and the style of clothing and the home suggests that Whitfield may have been one of these more prosperous rent farmers.

Arkansas History Commission, Little Rock

This unknown family had their picture taken outside one of the company houses at the lumber town of Rosboro in Clark County. They, like many other Arkansans, found new opportunities for employment away from agriculture in the developing industries of turn-of-the-century Arkansas.

Esidor Tiger, surrounded by his family at Luxora in 1904, was a member of Arkansas's growing merchant class. Tiger had come to the United States from Russia in 1897 to join his brother, Nathan, and Ike Levine in operating a general merchandise store that provided everything "From the Cradle to the Grave" to the residents of Manila. Tiger's actual name, Tager, had been changed when he entered the United States at Ellis Island.

M. Gordon Tiger

Labor's Many Faces

Farming remained the principal economic activity of most Arkansans during the revolutionary years of the New South. Tenants and field hands in Pulaski County are shown here harvesting the annual cotton crop in 1915 as it had been gathered for decades—by hand.

Bernie Babcock Collection, Arkansas
History Commission, Little Rock

Ed Kraus was a conductor on the Fort Smith and Western Railroad.
He and his crew are shown outside of Fort Smith in 1910.

University of Arkansas at Little Rock Libraries

William Prior Lee Cheshire is shown with his saw crew in the forests of Cleveland or Dallas County about 1915. These men were essential to the timber industry, clearing the forests and sending the fresh-cut logs to mills across the state for processing.
Arkansas History Commission, Little Rock

*These coal miners, employed by the Peerless Coal Company
at Paris, worked one of the state's deep mines in 1920.*

University of Arkansas at Little Rock Libraries

W. R. "Bud" Blesch, tended machinery at a thread mill at Barton in Phillips County. This picture, made in 1910, shows the change that was occurring in the work place as machinery became increasingly important in the economic activity of Arkansans.

Phillips County Museum

These hands on the drilling rig of the Bradstreet Laney No. 2 well near Smackover were part of the hundreds of oil-field workers who poured into southern Arkansas in the 1920s.
University of Arkansas at Little Rock Libraries

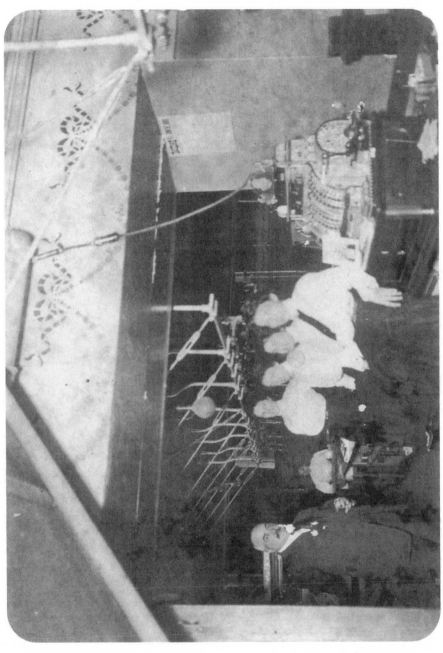

Representing changing occupational structures in the state, these retail clerks at Fort Smith in 1910 illustrate the increasing role of women in business.
University of Arkansas at Little Rock Libraries

Changing Surroundings

*At the turn of the century, despite significant changes, a few people
still lived much as others had decades earlier. This Ozark house
was typical of the homes not only of the people of the mountains
but also of thousands of other poor Arkansans throughout the state.*

Bernie Babcock Collection, Arkansas
History Commission, Little Rock

Log cabins still existed in Arkansas, but through the New South years material culture changed. The farm home of Henry Knockemous in Arkansas County was typical of prosperous farmers on the Grand Prairie in 1900. This style would have been common on the plains of Nebraska or Kansas. Arkansas History Commission, Little Rock

These rent houses in the small town of Amity in Clark County were representative of the types of homes known by hundreds of urban Arkansans. Inexpensive frame houses, often with rough board siding, could be thrown up quickly to meet the demands of new immigrants from the countryside.

Arkansas History Commission, Little Rock

Reflecting the most elaborate extreme, the Queen Anne–style home of J. H. Hornibrook,
built in Little Rock in 1888, nonetheless was typical of the types of houses built by
the successful merchants and professionals of the state's towns. Such structures reflected
the material success and the cultural aspirations of their inhabitants.

University of Arkansas at Little Rock Libraries

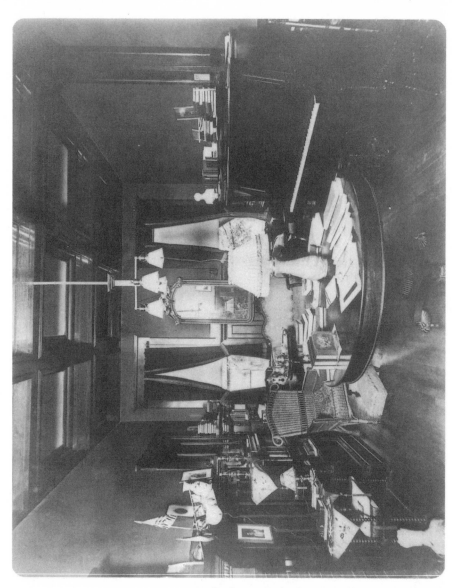

The piano studio of Ms. Jesse Turner of Fort Smith shows further the tastes of prosperous urban inhabitants. This picture, made in 1910, shows a room filled with the possessions that wealth made possible—not only a piano, but also good furniture, magazines and books, and even electric lights. The American flag suggests the increasing nationalism of such people in the South.

University of Arkansas at Little Rock Libraries

Commercial structures in the towns mimicked the buildings of larger cities and asserted a claim to urban identity. The buildings along Main Street in Hot Springs in 1905 were typical. Multistoried buildings, sometimes simple frame structures with cast-iron facades intended to create the appearance of more expensive and substantial materials such as stone, lined many Arkansas streets. Marking the transitional stage of this city, the roads remain unpaved.

University of Arkansas at Little Rock Libraries

Garrison Avenue at Fort Smith in 1905 shows how the technology of the new era had infringed upon the towns. Tracks for the city's trolley line ran down the center of the street under electrical lines that powered the cars. Telephone and power lines to businesses formed a web of wires overhead typical of most cities of the time.
University of Arkansas at Little Rock Libraries

From the isolation of the farm, the immigrant to town entered an environ-ment of congestion and noise. Crowds boarding a train at Little Rock present a typical scene of urban life at the turn of the century.
University of Arkansas at Little Rock Libraries

Urban culture even penetrated the countryside, as evidenced by this baseball team composed of tenants on a plantation near Conway.

Arkansas History Commission, Little Rock

Nothing represented the new era more than the introduction of machinery into the workplace. The huge cotton compress of the Little Rock Compress and Cotton Oil Company, dwarfing the workers around it, exemplified the job surroundings for more and more Arkansans during the New South years.

University of Arkansas at Little Rock Libraries

Plight of the Farmers

Industries that exploited Arkansas's timber and mineral resources along with the development of a fledgling manufacturing industry produced economic gains in Arkansas. For some areas the result was a previously unexperienced prosperity. For the state at large, however, problems associated with agriculture served as a brake on economic growth. Conditions obviously varied from farm to farm as there were major shifts and gains in some aspects of Arkansas's agricultural communities. Nonetheless, on the whole, worsening circumstances for farmers held back the state's promising march toward a better New South economy.

The railroads, responsible for new economic trends within the state, contributed greatly to the directions taken by agricultural Arkansas in the late nineteenth century. Product diversification and the opening of new lands for commercial agricultural development, both of which often interacted with one another, were among the positive aspects of the farm economy through these years, and the new rail lines were essential to both developments. As early as the late 1870s, visitors to the state reported an optimistic outlook for Arkansas agriculture and predicted future prosperity. A letter by a traveler printed in the St. Louis *Commercial Appeal* in 1877 found Arkansans to be more optimistic about the future than people in almost any other state and pointed to growth in the agricultural sector. It found new farmers, particularly those fleeing problems on the Great Plains, were bringing cash and new ideas about crops to the state. A farm revolution seemed imminent.

While overly optimistic, the 1877 letter accurately described the positive developments in local agriculture at the time. As the railroads expanded, they made possible the use of increasing amounts of land within the state for commercial farming. Railroad connections meant that land away from the river transportation arteries of the antebellum years now could get crops to market. Between 1880 and 1900, the amount of land being cultivated, that is in improved acres, statewide increased from 3,595,603 to 6,953,735 acres. The figures reflected a near doubling of productive farm lands.

At least part of this growth represented a movement into new regions. The Grand Prairie of the state was practically unoccupied at the end of the 1870s, bypassed by early farm settlers not only because of problems in transporting products but also because the clay soils were difficult to till and drain. During the 1880s the Rock Island Railroad vigorously promoted the settlement of the region by farmers from the prairies of Kansas, Nebraska, and Iowa. By the 1890s the area around Stuttgart became the center of large German communities recruited to settle there from the Midwest. Beginning in 1894 the National Slavonic Society and other organizations promoted the immigration of settlers from Pennsylvania to Prairie County, where they purchased farms and ultimately established Slovaktown. The result was that thousands of farmers moved into the Grand Prairie counties.

The farm economy of the region boomed. The number of improved acres reported for farms in Arkansas County increased almost 190 percent from 1880 to 1900, in Lonoke County by 141 percent, and in Prairie County by 155 percent. All three of these counties at the heart of the developing region outstripped the overall rate of growth in the state.

Also important for the general economy, Grand Prairie farmers experimented with new products when they found that cotton did not grow well there. Initially, much of the land was used for grazing as local farms specialized in livestock. Ultimately, the Midwesterners who moved into the region developed successful crops of wild and tame grasses that were mowed and baled for hay (much of which was sent by rail to Illinois for feeding out steers), winter oats, and other small grains. This innovation would continue, leading to the introduction of rice after the turn of the century.

The railroads also provided greater market access during these years to counties on the Ozark Plateau in the northwestern corner of the state.

During the 1880s, both the St. Louis and San Francisco and the Kansas City Southern pushed into Benton County. The Missouri and North Arkansas entered Arkansas in Carroll County and had reached Harrison by 1901, giving farmers in that area access to the St. Louis and San Francisco at Seligman, Missouri. The impact of these roads on farming in the northwest was almost immediate.

In 1880 not a single one of these counties had been among the top five producers of fruits and berries for market. By 1900 three of the top five, Washington, Benton, and Madison Counties, accounted for nearly 35 percent of all such goods grown in Arkansas. Apples, blackberries, cherries, grapes, peaches, pears, plums, and strawberries were among the new products grown there. As cider, dried fruit, vinegar, preserves, and even wine, these farm goods were shipped out on the new railroads to be sold in the national market.

As in the case of the development of the Grand Prairie, the opening of the northwest to greater economic activity was accompanied by social change as well. New peoples, typically from the northern states rather than from the South, steadily filtered in. Foreigners complimented the immigration. Perhaps the best known group would come at the turn of the century, when the remnants of an Italian agricultural community that had come to work on the Sunnyside Plantation in Chicot County in 1895 moved to Washington County, where they established Tontitown.

Even in the older agricultural areas of the state, the railroads encouraged farmers to experiment with raising new products. Railroad executives, just like the farmers themselves, saw benefits in diversification. If the price of cotton was down, that affected the railroads as well as the farmers. Orchard products did well in many areas of the state and attention focused to a considerable degree on them. The Iron Mountain Railroad, trying to increase traffic on their southwestern line, even operated a model farm near Hope in the 1890s to show farmers how to better cultivate various fruit trees.

The most important trend giving cause for optimism, however, was the steady increase in the production of cotton. The disruptions caused by the war were believed to be over, and prices seemed to have stabilized. Many hoped that this promised a return to the prosperity of the prewar years. Both in traditional areas of cultivation and regions where the crop had made few inroads prior to the 1870s, farmers placed greater emphasis upon raising cotton. The reason was simple. The railroads gave farmers access to market. Cotton was the one product with the greatest market value. If they decided to produce for the market, cotton was the inevitable choice, for it was the one thing that always had a cash demand.

In addition, the shift to cotton took place because it was the only cash crop familiar to most local farmers. Even in the antebellum years, small farmers outside of the plantation regions had always grown a little cotton that could be sold to get the money for those things they could not produce on the farm. It was not uncommon for the smallest farm in the mountain regions to have a modest cotton patch next to the house. As a result, farmers knew how to cultivate the crop, and when the market became accessible they simply increased the amount of their lands devoted to cotton. Everywhere the railroads went cotton followed, even out of the traditional plantation region and into the rest of the state.

The increasing importance of cotton on the state's farms could be seen especially in the amount of land devoted to it rather than to other crops. Census enumerators estimated that in 1879 of the over three million acres of harvested crops, 35 percent had been planted in cotton. The percentage of lands committed to cotton increased by 1889 to nearly four million acres, almost 45 percent of all harvested acres. During the 1890s this basic trend continued, although marketing weaknesses caused many farmers to try to secure greater self-sufficiency by committing more land to corn. Despite the slight reversals of the 1890s, cotton had significantly increased its hold on Arkansas farmers.

The immediate result of this massive use of farmland for cotton cultivation was that Arkansans grew more cotton than ever before. By 1880 the state's crop finally exceeded that of the last year before the Civil War when farmers produced 608,256 bales, nearly double the 367,393 harvested in 1860. Thereafter the number of bales continued to increase with 619,494 in 1890, and 709,880 in 1900. Through the 1880s and 1890s the harvest of all of the state's crops increased, but not at the same rate as cotton.

While in the late 1870s these trends appeared to promise a new abundance, the course of agricultural development through the rest of the century failed to produce the desired prosperity. Rather, Arkansas farmers confronted economic disaster during the 1880s. A variety of circumstances combined to produce a serious agricultural depression. Farmers, in many cases, sank into a grinding poverty that seemed to have no end. Agriculture appeared out of step with both the New Arkansas and the New South.

The farm crisis of the 1880s and 1890s was the result of the complicated interplay of many different forces. No one of these conditions may be said to have caused the problem, but central to this was the steady decline in the size of farms. The reason for this trend was simple. Good and even marginal agricultural land within the state was limited. The rural population, however, steadily increased as a result of both natural fertility and immigration. The opening of new lands created some new opportunities while the expansion of other industries created new jobs, but these were not enough to absorb the surplus population. Possessing limited skills and education that might have made them more mobile, the people of the countryside divided the land into smaller and smaller units. In 1880 the average farm size had been 128 acres. By 1900 it was only 93 acres.

The steady decrease in size made these farms less efficient and seriously affected the ability of the families that worked them to make any money. A farmer in 1900 working acreage nearly 30 percent smaller than in 1880 but with about the same number of people living on it, would have to increase its productivity by some 30 percent just to maintain the same financial level. He might increase productivity by using modern techniques and fertilizers, but as farms became smaller few operators had the money to afford such innovation. As late as 1900, for example, only 10 percent of Arkansas farmers used fertilizers. Crop rotation might have improved long-term yields, but small farmers could not afford to take any of their land out of productivity. Mechanization was almost nonexistent, with the typical farm still relying on mule-drawn plows that only cut relatively shallow furrows.

Unable to increase productivity with the use of improved techniques and forced to use their land year after year to grow cash crops, Arkansas farmers experienced an actual decline in productivity through the 1880s and 1890s. While the number of bales of cotton harvested increased, the actual number of bales produced per acre decreased. In 1879 the average cotton yield in the state had been .6 bales per acre. By the turn of the century this had dropped to .4 bales per acre. Corn yield also declined steadily, falling from nineteen bushels per acre in 1879 to only about sixteen bushels in 1899.

At the same time that farmers ran into problems caused by a reduction in acreage and diminishing productivity, their economic position was weakened further by steadily increasing costs. The introduction of railroad transportation into the state had made it possible for farmers to engage in commercial agriculture, but it had also increased their access to a wide variety of inexpensive goods. Throughout the state, farmers needed more and more cash as these store-bought goods became essential items for their households. As shown by an archaeological survey of the Moser family farmstead in southwestern Benton County, even families in the relatively isolated Ozarks were tied into trade networks that brought goods from all over the world into their homes. Chinaware from the Staffordshire potteries in England and companies in Ohio, glass canning jars manufactured by the Ball Company of Muncie, Indiana, and pharmaceutical bottles from various northern states were found on the Moser site. Nearby stores offered goods as varied as processed flour, coffee, overalls, calico, laces, millinery, ribbons, dry goods, women's clothing, kerosene, coal oil, knives, and farm machinery. Rural families remained careful consumers, but at the same time their purchases, often using credit, increased. The price of such goods raised the cost of living and helped to undermine potential profits.

Increasing consumption of store-bought manufactured goods cost the farm family in ways other than the simple retail price of the merchandise they bought. Especially for those who operated on a credit basis, buying more products at the store meant that more money had to be borrowed during the year. That meant the farmer had to pay the cost of financing credit and, thus, increased operating costs for the year. Even when merchants were honest, farmers who bought goods on credit paid higher prices than they would have if they had been able to pay cash. Country merchants usually marked up the price of goods sold on credit at least 25 percent, though often higher. While rural consumers believed this meant they were paying exorbitant prices and were being cheated, merchants argued that the higher rate for credit purchases was necessary. They found many farmers unable to pay their debts and the higher prices helped cover such risks. Whether justified or not, many observers blamed the system of credit for causing rural families to overspend and leaving them in debt at the end of the year.

The situation was worsened, particularly in the case of African-American tenants and sharecroppers, by the open abuses that infected the system of farm finance. There was nothing inherently unfair in the existing credit scheme, but it contained no effective safeguards for debtors. The contracts involved relationships between one party with considerable power and another without any. Exact contractual arrangements were usually verbal and the creditor kept the books. Many debtors believed that their creditors always made sure that end-of-the-year accountings came out in their favor, adding charges for goods not received or for services never provided. By the time all advances had been paid back and charges had been settled, the borrower often had nothing left or worse, a future debt to pay. If the debtor was illiterate or unable to do simple arithmetic, it was difficult to question the figures of his creditor. Even if cheating could be proved, however, resolution of a dispute would have been in a court, where even more money would be needed. In effect, the debtor had no recourse but to accept the situation brought about at the end of each harvest.

Adding to this burden was the fact that farming, by its very nature, was a risky business. Many conditions essential to a good crop year did not work in favor of the farmer during the 1880s and 1890s. Weather, which always played a major role in success or failure in agricultural Arkansas, was one of these factors. Too much rain in the spring or a late frost could destroy a crop just coming up. At times, spring floods literally washed away fields. Too much rain during the summer kept farmers out of the fields and allowed weeds to overgrow crops. Too little rain stunted plant growth, while rain in the fall could delay a harvest and destroy a crop still out in the field.

Historically, the 1870s were relatively good weather years, but the 1880s were marked by a series of natural disasters. Beginning in the summer and autumn of 1881, farmers faced the first serious drought since immediately after the Civil War. This was followed in the winter and spring of 1882 by heavy rains and flooding that first delayed planting and then washed away what had been put in. Many were left destitute as a result of the 1882 flood, and farmers were forced to secure additional loans to buy new seeds to put in another crop. Throughout the rest of the 1880s and into the 1890s, cold wet springs, unwanted rains, and extended dry spells periodically visited the state and undercut farm productivity.

If the weather was not problem enough, farmers also faced a constant struggle against plant diseases and insect pests, and these appeared particularly threatening during this time. Cool wet springs exacted a toll by encouraging rust and blight. Wet autumns rotted cotton bolls, and bad weather especially aided insect pests. Aphids, ants, army worms, caterpillars, and bollworms could appear in a field any time from late spring until the fall. From about 1887 onward, bollworms appeared regularly in Arkansas fields in July, destroying what farmers envisioned as bumper crops. Prior to modern fungicides and pesticides, the farmer could do little to avert the destruction. Wealthier planters began experimentation by the 1880s with various powdered insecticides such as Paris green, prepared from arsenic trioxide and acetate of copper, and London purple to fight worms. Most, however, could not afford these early pesticides, and invariably harvests in the 1880s and 1890s were reduced by the ravages of disease and insects.

If all the difficulties encountered by farmers in the last decades of the nineteenth century were not enough, the final blow to their efforts came as farm prices experienced a general decline. Prices softened during the 1880s, then collapsed in the midst of a widespread economic depression in the 1890s. The causes for this drop were largely beyond the farmers' control. Domestic overproduction was a factor, with cotton supplies recovering from the effects of the Civil War by the 1880s, and corn and wheat booming with the opening of new lands on the Great Plains. The effect of overproduction was aggravated, however, by changing world markets. During the 1860s rival cotton-producing areas had emerged elsewhere in the world, particularly in India and Egypt, that competed with the South. The amount of cotton available outpaced the needs of manufacturers. Farmers growing corn and wheat faced competition in world markets too: the opening of farm lands in Australia and South America adversely affected American grain exports.

Prices began to plummet after 1880 for all of the state's important cash crops. The fall was all the more disastrous because farms had shifted from subsistence or mixed operations to a greater emphasis on these products. The decline in cotton prices was particularly damaging, and there seemed to be no bottom to the fall. In 1865 the wholesale price of cotton had been 83 cents a pound, nearly eight times the 11 cents a pound it had brought in 1860. These prices had encouraged many Arkansans to go back into cotton production when the war ended and had helped establish it as the primary cash crop among Arkansas farmers. By 1870 cotton prices had dipped to 24 cents, much less than the immediate postwar high, but still enough to make a profit. By 1880 cotton fell to prewar levels, and farmers believed it had steadied. In 1886, however, prices fell to 9.4 cents and then began a downward spiral that took it to a low of 6 cents a pound in 1898.

For those whose primary cash crop was something other than cotton, the economic situation was just as bad. Prices plunged to all-time lows. The problem was not just overproduction. Wheat and corn producers traditionally had sent their goods to local markets that were protected from serious competition. However, the railroads forced local farmers to compete with others throughout the nation; many could not. Wheat flour made from crops grown on mechanized farms in the Midwest and milled in major centers such as Minneapolis sold cheaper than locally grown and milled goods. In many cases, local farmers could not even make a profit by matching these prices.

Both wheat and corn prices tumbled downward drastically, just as in the case of cotton. Wheat dropped from $1.37 per bushel in 1870 to $1.06 in

1880 and then to $0.89 in 1890. Prices bottomed out at $0.60 per bushel in 1895. Corn suffered the same precipitous decline in price. Averaging 40.9 cents a bushel between 1878 and 1881, prices dropped to an average of 39.8 cents between 1882 and 1885, then to 35.9 cents between 1886 and 1899. In the years 1890–1893, prices rose to a 41.7 average, then collapsed to 29.7 cents during the next three years.

Theoretically, farmers who faced such conditions might change crops or devote more of their resources to producing goods that would make them self-sufficient. The system of farm finance, however, restricted such flexibility and helped to ensure that they would continue to grow the major cash crops. When money lenders sought agricultural collateral for the loans they made, they wanted a product that had a sure market. There were few crops that had the same value as cotton, corn, and wheat, even at their low prices. To borrow the money necessary to begin the crop year, farmers inevitably had to agree to cultivate one of these crops. Some might experiment with diversification, but few could secure the financing to do so. Most producers, well aware of the problems with commodity prices, had no choice but to settle up at the end of each year's failure, return to the landowner or country merchant to secure more credit, then plant cotton, corn, or wheat, hoping that the weather, insects, plant diseases, and prices would break right and allow them to make a profit.

The most obvious economic result through these years was the steady expansion of tenant farming and the proportional decline in farms worked by their actual owners. At least in part this took place because of foreclosures by creditors. By 1882 newspapers reported that merchants and bankers were seizing farm properties to fulfill unpaid debts. In such cases, the owner might even continue to work his old farm, though as a tenant. In addition, the number of tenants increased because few young people or newcomers had the economic resources to buy land. The only way for them to work was as tenants. At the same time, particularly in the Delta, some lands were being taken up by out-of-state corporate interests whose presence limited further access to the land by individuals. Across the state, merchants, bankers, and even corporations, rather than actual farm operators, became the new landlords.

The increase in farm tenantry was firmly established in the 1880s, but during the 1890s almost two decades of debts produced a major shift in agricultural operations within the state. In 1880 the United States Census Bureau had reported that 30.91 percent of farms in Arkansas were worked by tenants. By 1890 that number had increased to 32.11 percent. At the turn of the century, when nationally only 35.3 percent of farms were operated by tenants, 45.4 percent of those in Arkansas were tenant operated. The number of farms not worked by their actual owners in 1900 ranged from 87 percent in Crittenden County to 21 percent in Van Buren County.

In addition to the simple expansion of tenantry, the loss of independent farms saw more and more whites integrated into what had initially been a system largely for blacks. By 1900, while 74 percent of black farmers were tenants, 35 percent of white farmers operated as tenants. In absolute numbers, white tenants outnumbered blacks, with some 46,178 whites working as either cash or share tenants compared with 34,962 blacks. In 1900, white tenantry existed in the old plantation counties, such as Mississippi County where 56 percent of white farmers were tenants. It was also pervasive in the mountainous counties of the northwest, as in Yell County where the rate was 51 percent of white farmers.

Landowning and tenant farmers found little relief from the government in their struggle for survival. By the 1880s differences in debtor and creditor interests were sharpened. In 1883 the general assembly strongly reinforced the hand of creditors by amending the mortgage laws of the state to ensure that farm owners and tenants who had borrowed money would pay. New legislation made a mortgagee's failure to carry out a contract a criminal offense and the basis for forfeiting all property. No protection was offered, however, against any abuses of the creditor.

The farm crisis was much more, however, than simple economic hard times: it represented a widespread social disaster. Families entered into an era of destitution. Social tensions increased within rural communities. Rural folks and their communities stagnated, unable to change. The situation had overwhelmed them and added little to the vitality of the overall economic and social innovation in the state.

Years of poverty left many tenant families with no resources at all. On many farms tenants lived in two-room shacks provided by the landlord— one room for cooking and eating and the other in which the entire family slept. These homes were often constructed of green pine lumber, and after a year or two holes between the planks hardly kept the weather out. If they had any furniture at all, it was usually homemade. Cooking utensils seldom amounted to much more than an all-purpose iron pot. Observing tenant life in northeastern Arkansas, Octave Thanet noted that sometimes "the renter will have nothing beyond his grimy hands and the rags on his back."

Poverty ultimately was more than a simple lack of material goods. A study of the Cedar Grove community in Lafayette County, the report of an archaeological examination of the skeletal remains of those buried in the Cedar Grove cemetery around the turn of the century, offers insights into the lives of members of a typical African-American tenant farmer community. Located along the Red River, during the antebellum years the Cedar Grove area had been the site of large cotton plantations. As elsewhere in the postwar years, the land had been divided up among tenants. Cedar Grove, the location of a Baptist church, became a small community where many of these families worshipped and were buried.

In many respects, the diet of the Cedar Grove inhabitants was worse than that of slaves. A variety of bone abnormalities indicate that most of the people of Cedar Grove consumed a diet that was low in vitamins B, C, and D, deficient in iron, and lacking in protein. These characteristics would be typical in a person who primarily consumed corn (typically as hominy or corn bread) and pork (usually fat bacon or salt pork), which were the mainstays of poor blacks and whites. While this diet was at times supplemented with wild game and fish, other vegetables and fruits were hard to obtain, and in the midst of economic difficulties, broadening the diet was even more difficult. This produced serious health problems among the residents of Cedar Grove.

Some diseases were directly caused by the inadequate diet. Weaning diarrhea, often fatal, resulted from protein malnutrition that occurred among children at the time they were taken off breast milk and put on amino acid–deficient foods. Pellagra, caused by a deficiency of niacin (one of the B vitamins), produced a variety of skin problems, nervous conditions, digestive problems such as diarrhea, and eventually mental disorders.

When combined with poor sanitary conditions, malnutrition made it possible for other diseases to wreak havoc. Tuberculosis, the leading cause of death in the state when the health department began keeping statistics in 1914, was apparent in the Cedar Grove community. Pneumonia and other respiratory illnesses were widespread.

Statewide, poverty clearly added to the prevalence of disease. The evidence from Cedar Grove does not show the extent that other diseases preyed upon poor farming communities, but a variety of studies from the turn of the century do. Many rural Arkansans suffered from typhoid fever, contracted through contaminated drinking water. Studies of rural wells in the early twentieth century indicated that as many as 50 percent of them contained harmful bacteria. In lowland areas malaria was pervasive. Usually called the chills or fever, malaria did not exact a high death toll itself but weakened its sufferers, making them susceptible to other diseases. Hookworm was another environmental hazard. A parasite living in the ground, the hookworm invaded a human host usually by entry through the sole of the foot. The small worm eventually attached itself in the intestines where it lived on blood and tissue fluids. In victims badly infested, hookworms produced symptoms of lethargy, a characteristic often attributed to the Southern poor, stunted growth, and could actually lead to death. Early medical studies by the Rockefeller Hookworm Commission found that nearly 20 percent of Arkansans were infected, and in some of the counties in the southern part of the state the number was as great as 50 percent.

These maladies did not respect wealth or class, but to a large extent they represented environmental hazards that hit the poor hardest. Well-to-do people could find safe sources of water. Wealthier families knew of the threat of malaria and often avoided exposure by trips to the mountains at the height of the season. If infected, they could use quinine to relieve symptoms. Hookworm had an easy solution: wear shoes. For many poor farm families, however, it was impossible to escape the surroundings that confronted them with all of these problems. Shoes were often a luxury, and children, especially during the summer, were expected to go barefoot.

Overall, the cost of poverty and disease was enormous, particularly in deaths among members of the rural community. Infant and child mortality rates were particularly high. Across the state in 1880, seventy-four out of every one thousand newborn children died before they reached the age of one, a death rate of nearly 10 percent. At Cedar Grove, the infant mortality rate was closer to 30 percent. Survival of infancy, however, led only to a hard life and an early death for adults. In this highly stressed agricultural community life expectancy probably was only about forty years. The price of poverty was high.

Another result of the economic situation in the 1880s and 1890s was heightened social tensions. It appeared in the form of growing class hostilities but more often in the form of racial conflict. African-Americans in particular often believed that their impoverishment was due not only to economic conditions but also to the efforts of white landowners to cheat them. Through the 1880s and 1890s blacks in the Mississippi River Delta counties and along the Arkansas River Valley protested unfair treatment. Some tried to pressure landowners by threatening to leave the country. At times, with little chance of securing redress in the justice system, they acted violently. The burning of farm structures or equipment was one means of getting back at the landlord whom they believed had wronged them. Inevitably such protests led to even further violence and often to the death of African-Americans. Between 1882 and 1903, reported lynchings ended the lives of 139 blacks in Arkansas.

An outburst of violence in Lee County in 1891 was fairly typical of such events. That year cotton pickers who were part of the Colored Farmers Alliance became involved in a dispute with local farmers over wages, demanding that they be paid 75 cents per hundred pounds rather than the 50 cents local planters had agreed to. Ultimately, the pickers staged a strike and in the ensuing dispute burned several gins in the county. For the laborers, the protest settled little as local authorities responded with a heavy hand. A posse, deputized by the county sheriff after the attacks upon property and the murder of a plantation manager, went after the men they suspected of supporting the protest. When the sheriff arrested nine of the strike leaders, a mob of masked white men seized and hanged them. Before the violence was over, fifteen African-Americans were killed.

Rising social tensions also appeared in the form of conflict between blacks and poor whites. The latter often perceived the introduction of African-American tenants into a community as a particular threat to their economic position. They feared that black tenants would make it more difficult for whites to get land to farm, plus drive down the value of their labor. In 1882 the Little Rock and Fort Smith Railroad precipitated problems in western Arkansas when they began trying to create African-American agricultural communities along its line west of Little Rock. When black farmers attempted to move into southern Van Buren County in 1883, they were met with death threats. Nightriders raided their homes and ordered them to leave the area immediately. In 1885 men dressed in the regalia of the Reconstruction Ku Klux Klan harassed blacks in Conway County and Pope County, killing one African-American who had attempted to farm there. As economic conditions worsened, nightriding against black farmers took place across the state, with churches burned, homes shot into, and lives threatened. While authorities seldom arrested or prosecuted anyone for these episodes and the precise cause of such attacks can only be guessed, the correlation between the violence and economic problems suggests that the latter played a major role in the creation of social tension.

For the majority of Arkansas farmers, the situation in the 1880s and 1890s must have been all the more frustrating because there appeared to be no way out. Their options were limited: they might leave agriculture, they might migrate out of the state or even the nation, or they could simply move on to new farms elsewhere. Conditions that existed meant that of these options, the majority could do little but stay where they were.

The ability of families to leave farming to take advantage of other types of economic activity was restricted to a considerable degree by their lack of education. Inadequate schools and schooling clearly worked to ensure that each new generation of farm children was doomed to continued poverty. The reasons rural children were not educated well were simple enough. Their opportunities to go to school were limited. At the turn of the century, rural schools generally ran no longer than five months, when town schools already operated for nine. The year was usually broken up into two terms, one starting after crops had been laid by in mid-July and running until the September harvest, and the other following the harvest and lasting until late January, when farmers turned to clearing ground in preparation for new crops. Classes were small, with older students often teaching the younger ones. Teaching materials, including books, were often inadequate. Teachers were poorly prepared for their tasks.

The reasons for this substandard education were complex, but the direct cause of school problems was inadequate financing. To change school conditions would have cost money, and rural schools lagged far behind those of the towns and of the rest of the nation. At the turn of the century, the public schools of Little Rock, Fort Smith, and Hot Springs spent approximately eighteen dollars per student for schools, while nationally state spending for schools was twenty-eight dollars. However, spending on rural schools was a mere fraction of these disbursements, with the average throughout the state being only about seven dollars per student.

The failure to properly finance schools reflected an intricate set of circumstances that underlay educational problems. Arkansas had created a public school system in the 1870s that had placed financial support primarily on local school districts. This made raising money difficult. Towns and cities often possessed both the interest in providing schools and the tax base to finance them, but in the countryside taxpayers often perceived schools and school taxes as worsening an already difficult economic situation. For those merchants and landowners who might have been able to afford the taxes, schools were seen as institutions that would only disrupt their labor force.

Support for schools even lagged among families with children whose education could have been a long-term benefit. If the family was barely making enough money to support itself year to year, it was hard to agree to raising school taxes. Further, schools interfered with the field work of children, cutting into the economic well-being of the family. In Arkansas's urban schools, the average student attended classes 74 percent of the time. In the countryside, a student attending half of the classes was considered average. Lagging attendance reflected the lack of support among the parents of school-aged children for the whole educational effort. With a lack of support both from propertied interests and the families of students themselves, the failure of local districts to improve the rural schools is hardly surprising.

For whatever reason, the chances that a rural child could receive a good education were low, and the social price paid by poor Arkansans was immense. It consisted of a persisting problem of illiteracy and inferior math skills, all of which produced an immobile rural population. The census showed that in 1879, 28.8 percent of Arkansans ten years of age or older could not read and 38 percent were unable to write. Inadequate education had even more dire results among the state's poorer citizens. Among the same age group of African-Americans, most of whom could be considered poor, over 75 percent were unable to write. In the same census, the number unable to read and write in Massachusetts was 5.3 and 6.5 percent respectively. Some progress was made in the next two decades but at the turn of the century the number of whites who could not write stood at approximately 12 percent and the number of African-Americans at 43 percent. Census takers did not bother with math knowledge, but later studies of rural schools showed that the skills of their pupils typically lagged behind those of students in the towns and elsewhere in the nation.

For the rural Arkansas poor, this meant that each generation would inevitably be forced back into the farm labor pool, back into the tenant system with all of its economic problems. Even if they eventually could move to town and away from the farm, they would not have the skills to acquire good jobs. A twentieth-century educational report cited serious consequences in the lack of education for the rural poor and concluded: "To be born in Arkansas is a misfortune and an injustice from which they will never recover and upon which they will look back with bitterness when plunged, in adult life, into competition with the children born from other states."

If they were unable to move to the towns to secure jobs in the new industries, some farm families sought to break their cycle of poverty by leaving the state. At least a few African-Americans responded to the grinding poverty on the tenant farms and the violence that they faced by fleeing, seeking opportunities on new grounds. Back-to-Africa schemes developed periodically throughout these years, usually with potential emigrants considering a move to Liberia. Others with more realistic expectations hoped to find new homes in Kansas or in the Oklahoma Territory. Only a few took such a course, however. Relocation required money that the majority of African-Americans did not have, and most potential emigrants quickly soured on the idea after newspapers reported that the agents and promoters of such schemes were unscrupulous men who took their money and never got them to their destination. Ironically, at the same time that many African-Americans tried to leave Arkansas, others were coming to the state, trying to escape similar economic problems in the older Southern states to the east.

For the majority of Arkansas's rural poor, white and black, the only option was to stay on the farm. When deep enough in debt, many tenants packed up their belongings and walked away during the night. Landowners and merchants seldom tried to track them down or prosecute them for failing to pay their debts. The tenant simply moved to the next neighborhood or to the next county and tried again. The steady movement of these tenants, farm to farm, year after year, indicated the difficulties all had in achieving financial success.

Historians have debated the basic question of how Arkansas and other Southern states became involved in an agriculturally based economy that offered little flexibility or reward. It is clear that it was the product of a large number of forces which were not only at work in Arkansas but also in agricultural communities throughout the nation. A variety of natural and market forces played a role in creating agrarian problems. While the modern student may recognize the complexity of the situation, contemporaries looked for other explanations, for clear and simple answers to their plight. Increasingly, they searched for someone to blame for what was taking place. By the 1880s the rural problems had produced a major movement that sought solutions to the plight of the farmers and placed demands on government to help achieve that goal.

Working Class Protest in the New Arkansas

The struggle to produce a New South, with its consequent social upheaval produced by urbanization, an agricultural depression, and heightened tensions in rural communities, provided fertile ground for discontent. Arkansans, initially unsure about the causes for the economic problems and turmoil they saw, began to ask why these things were happening. Many joined in organizations that were designed to help them deal with this new world. Ultimately, rural Arkansans embraced political reform as the means of helping themselves. The politics of change produced new parties and a challenge to the Democratic Party's control over state government. The political conflict left the Democrats in power, but not without the end result of progressive development. Even where conservatives marshaled massive forces to maintain the status quo, conditions in the Arkansas of the 1880s and 1890s produced continuing change.

Rural communities were the source of the first organized efforts to understand and handle the problems that seemed to be overwhelming farmers. Historians have seen a unified farm movement emerging, but in fact every community seemed to have its own idea about what the cause of the problem was and how to solve it. Farmers joined state and national organizations, but they remained remarkably independent in their judgments and actions. This fact makes following the historical threads of farm protest difficult and compels the historian to tell their story through the larger organizations. It is important to realize, however, that each of these groups represented very complex and constantly changing coalitions. At various times planters, yeoman farmers, and tenants, growing everything from cotton to grapes, constituted the base for these organizations.

The first widely publicized farm group to appear in Arkansas was the Grange, or the Order of the Patrons of Husbandry. The Grange, founded in 1867, was a national organization that emphasized education as the path to improving agricultural conditions. Local granges in Arkansas had appeared in the early 1870s, and on June 18, 1873, these combined to form the state Grange. Their selection of John Thompson Jones, a prominent cotton planter, as the head of this group indicated that Grange leaders saw farm problems as applicable to all classes: rich and poor had to cooperate. The Arkansas Grange embraced the educational ideas of the national organization, but along with other state groups it increasingly criticized banks, railroads, and middle men as the real culprits in the farmers' problems. Their solution was to cut out middle men as much as possible with the formation of farm cooperatives. Although avowedly nonpolitical, they also sought legislation restricting the power of monopolies such as the railroads. The state organization grew rapidly and by October 1875 claimed 20,471 members and 631 subordinate granges across the state.

The Grange movement lasted for only a short time in Arkansas. Supporters found it difficult to set up cooperatives. The legislature paid little attention to their requests for restrictions on railroads or other corporations the Grange considered monopolistic. Political candidates from the Democratic and Republican Parties readily endorsed Grange goals in campaigns but seldom pushed them if elected. Political frustration may explain why the movement peaked so quickly in the state. By 1876 the number of local chapters and members in the Grange began to decline. As a local organization, the Grange continued to exist into the twentieth century, but it disappeared as a state-wide force among farmers. Many of its leaders moved on to other organizations, often advocating greater political activism and the need for farmers to form a third party if they were ever to be able to secure their goals.

The first stop in their challenge to the political status quo for many former Grange leaders was the Greenback Party, which ran candidates for local office in the 1878 elections. The core membership of the Arkansas Greenback Party were disgruntled farmers, and its leadership drew heavily from the Grange. The party took its name and platform from the National Greenback Party, which had organized and then run a presidential candidate in 1876. The platform focused on the monetary policy of the federal government as the chief culprit in economic problems. That policy, which held the national currency to a gold standard, produced a deflation that farmers, indeed all debtors, concluded worked unfairly on them. The Greenbackers wanted paper currency expanded to end deflation and, hopefully, to cut the cost of credit.

Farm problems were not linked so simply to any single part of the national economy, but monetary policy unquestionably played a role in producing them. Even if farmers and their leaders realized the problem was more complex, the Greenback panacea was a good starting point. Furthermore, it provided a simple issue upon which support could be rallied and the power of the Democratic Party challenged. Farmers gave strong support to the fledgling party, as did leaders and members of the labor unions forming in the state at that same time.

The Greenbackers ran their first state campaign in 1880, when they nominated W. P. "Buck" Parks for governor against the Democratic nominee, former treasurer Thomas J. Churchill. Parks ran a strong campaign, appealing to Republican voters in the state for support as well as members of the Grange. Even though he lost, the results indicated that a political change in Arkansas might be possible. Parks's 31,284 votes amounted to over 27 percent of the total cast. It was clear that a sizable minority of voters were ready for change.

Like the Grange, the Greenback-Labor Party's life was relatively short. In 1882 it nominated Rufus K. Garland, brother of United States Senator Augustus H. Garland and longtime political outsider, for governor. Garland could not secure Republican backing in 1882 because that party ran its own candidate, William D. Slack. Democrat James H. Berry won easily. By the next election, political forces were moving in new directions, leaving the Greenback-Labor Party behind.

From 1882 to 1884, worsening conditions for farmers caused a proliferation of new farm organizations and the development of a new political militancy. The most significant of these, given its role during the next years, was the Agricultural Wheel, organized as the Wattensas Farmer's Club in Prairie County on February 15, 1882. By 1883 it had spread to much of the rest of the state, and the local groups established the Arkansas Wheel. Other farm groups included the Brothers of Freedom formed in Johnson County, the Sons of Liberty, the Farmers' Club, the Farmers' Union, and the Reform Society.

All of these organizations shared an analysis of the farm problem similar to that advanced by the Grange. In addition, these farming groups sought to help themselves by educating members about ways to cut costs and bring up crop prices. The first could be achieved by avoiding debt, producing as much on the farm as possible to avoid buying it from merchants. The second was possible if farmers reduced the production of the main cash crops and invested in diversification.

Increasingly, however, these new groups considered farmers to be the victims of capitalists, who purposefully or through ignorance exploited them, and national and state governments. They perceived themselves as working hard, living economical lives, and yet still being unable to educate their children or have anything other than the bare means to pay off their debts. At the same time lawyers, bankers, merchants, and railroad men made enormous sums of money and lived lives of comfort. Farmers concluded that something was seriously wrong, because they were the heart of the community and were receiving nothing for their labor.

Since they believed the government had been taken from them, farmers increasingly considered the necessity of political action, although they would vigorously debate whether they should operate through existing parties or a new farm party. Few doubted the need to secure government that favored their interests. The national Grange earlier had put forward the basic agrarian legislative agenda when it proposed regulation of banking and transportation to ensure fair interest rates and shipping costs. This legislative program was expanded by the new farm groups. In addition, some farm leaders concluded that to gain any of their goals they would have to remove what they considered an entrenched political elite from power. In Arkansas, rural politics threatened to become not just a fight between farmers and financial and transportation corporations, but one between farmers and the Democratic Party.

By 1884 the Greenback-Labor Party was dead, but nothing had emerged to replace it. Farm groups remained unsure whether or not they should engage in politics, although some acted. Local chapters of the Brothers of Freedom decided to run their own tickets in some counties. In Johnson, Newton, and Van Buren Counties, their candidates swept to power, taking most local offices. Partial victories were won by the Brothers in Franklin, Perry, Pope, and Searcy Counties. A combination with Republicans brought fusion candidates to power in Crawford and Scott Counties. The Agricultural Wheel preferred to push pro-Wheel candidates within the Democratic Party, unsuccessfully supporting John G. Fletcher of Little Rock for the gubernatorial nomination. During the organization's state convention in

July 1884, following Fletcher's failure to secure the nomination, Republicans approached Wheel leaders about the possibility of a fusion ticket. The leadership decided to stay out of the election and to continue working through the existing parties.

With the merger of the Brothers of Freedom and the Agricultural Wheel in 1885, however, steps were made toward creating a much more militant farm organization that viewed independent political action as necessary. The organization created by the combination was called the Agricultural Wheel, but from the beginning the leadership of the new group came from the Brothers of Freedom. Leaders of the Brothers had always been more radical and more political than those of the Wheel, and their influence directed its course. In 1886 Isaac McCracken of Ozone, originally a leader of the Brothers of Freedom and an ardent supporter of independent political action, was elected president of the state Wheel. At the state convention at Little Rock June 8-11, McCracken succeeded in persuading the membership to nominate candidates for the upcoming elections despite strong internal opposition. Initially, John G. Fletcher received the gubernatorial nomination, but he later withdrew and was replaced by Charles E. Cunningham of Little Rock, a successful businessman who had been an active Greenbacker in 1876 and 1882. The Wheel had entered politics.

The organization's 1886 platform presented the details of the political agenda that had been developed during the previous two years. It began with the general principle that the organization believed it was time that "the rights and privileges of the people shall no longer be trampled upon by monopoly," then went on to state specific reforms they desired. Some of their demands had to do with national policy, in which they wanted public lands turned over to actual settlers rather than corporations, the abolition of national banks, a government currency, reduction in tariffs, and a graduated income tax. Regarding state matters, they called for regulation of rates, bond issues, and collection of back taxes on railroads; reform of road laws to make them less burdensome; a prohibition amendment; an enforceable usury law; tax assessments to be made at the township level; and an end to leasing convict labor that competed with free labor.

The Democrats, who were running Simon P. Hughes for reelection, clearly saw the Wheel campaign as a threat. They moved to co-opt many of the agrarians' issues, including demands for tariff reduction, an expanded currency, railroad regulation, and revisions of the state's tax system. The resulting Democratic platform was quite similar to that put forth by the Wheel.

As Wheel and Democratic candidates adopted similar positions, the question for voters who wanted change was which party's candidates could be trusted better to carry out this program. In a relatively trouble-free election, the decision of voters was mixed. Hughes handily defeated Cunningham, 90,649 votes to only 19,069. The Republican candidate, Lafayette Gregg, received 54,064 votes. Results in the legislative elections were less clear. Cunningham claimed that between thirty and thirty-five Wheelers had been elected to the legislature, suggesting that farmers might expect some legislation to be introduced favorable to their demands for reform. Others, however, placed the number much lower.

Whether pushed by the Wheel presence or simply trying to appease the agrarian dissidents, the Democratic majority in the 1887 General Assembly did make some effort at addressing the problems that concerned these groups, but the continued power of conservative Democrats in both houses ensured caution among the legislators. This assembly ended the practice of public officials accepting free passes from railroads and imposed additional restrictions on the lines. Laws provided for a three dollar tax per mile on sleeping cars used in the state; fixed passenger rates at three cents per mile; prohibited the consolidation, lease, or purchase of parallel competing railroad lines; prohibited interlocking directorates for competing lines; prohibited discrimination in charges for transportation; stopped the practice of "pooling" freight; required printed rate schedules; provided for the collection of overdue corporate taxes; enabled the constitutional provision prohibiting usury; and limited the time for filing suits under mortgages.

At the same time, the legislature rejected the creation of a railroad commission, which had become an issue during the campaign. It also ignored numerous other agrarian demands such as the creation of a bureau of agriculture and labor statistics. While willing to control the operations of large corporations, the general assembly was unwilling to do anything that would have required an increase in state expenditures and, subsequently, state taxes. As they offered something of an olive branch, the Democratic legislature ignored most of the Wheel's program and provided its supporters with plenty of reasons to be dissatisfied.

Following the failure of the Wheel program in the general assembly, the organization's leaders backed the formation of a permanent third party. In addition, they reached out to others in order to broaden their political base. Among these were African-American farmers, many of whom already had formed their own segregated farm organizations at the local level. In 1887 the Agricultural Wheel seated a black delegation from St. Francis County in its state convention, signaling a revolutionary change in Arkansas's political dynamics and presenting a serious threat to the political status quo. The development of a biracial coalition allowed agrarian leaders to make a clear appeal to class, calling for support from poor and yeoman farmers of both races seeking political changes that would ease their desperate plight. While such an appeal risked the support of well-to-do farmers, this combination represented a potential majority of voters. If it could hold together, political power could be exercised directly in their interest.

In addition, Wheel leaders approached members of the newly developing labor movement in the hopes of broadening their base even further. The agrarian portion of the state's population was not the only place where economic and social change produced discontent. Workers, particularly those in the developing new industries, had their own concerns and were organizing too. Unions had existed within Arkansas prior to the 1870s, but were typically crafts unions and not part of any broader national movement. Typographers, carpenters, painters, stonemasons, and tailors existed in the urban areas. New groups, similarly organized, appeared in the 1870s. Sheet-iron workers, machinists, and boilermakers represented typical union organizations associated with the state's railroad and industrial enterprises. Some miners in the western coal fields also formed unions during these years. Local in organization and outlook, these unions served as social organizations for their members and also staged an occasional strike to force employers to respond to wage or other demands.

Although the economic situation of most workers connected with the railroads or the new industries appeared to be considerably better than that of farmers, their protests and strikes indicated that several issues concerned them. The most common grievance centered on wages, despite the fact that these were relatively better than what they could get on the farm. Workers, however, often argued that the money was still not appropriate to the intensity or the danger involved in their jobs. In addition, these men were concerned with job security and especially with any attempt, such as the use of convict labor, to replace them or undermine their wage position.

It is hard to know all of the reasons for these labor grievances. Contemporary newspapers paid little attention to union activity. Little Rock papers were concerned when their typographers struck for better wages in 1876, but throughout the years from 1875 to 1884 strikes were infrequently mentioned in their columns. Even then, full information was not provided.

Throughout the nation, however, manufacturing workers had deep concerns about the new circumstances in which they found themselves. The nature of work was becoming different. Bosses were no longer owners but managers. Social benefits that were part of the day-to-day business of a small company disappeared as larger businesses moved to more rational systems of management. Skilled labor often gave way to unskilled labor as machinery increasingly did the job of people. The new workplace, surrounded by machinery that could mangle and boilers that could explode, was even more dangerous than the farm. Especially for workers brought up in the countryside, the changed world must have seemed threatening.

In the economic downturn of the early 1880s, conditions worsened and the move toward organized labor actions against employers increased. A sharp escalation in conflict took place in April 1883, when brakemen on the Iron Mountain Railroad walked off the job after the company laid off one-third of their number. In their attempt to force concessions from the railroad, the workers tried to stop all trains from leaving the yards in North Little Rock. The strike was broken, although labor relations were not improved, when the Iron Mountain secured the support of the Pulaski County sheriff and a posse to move the trains and arrest anyone who tried to stop them. In the end, the railroad fired between sixty and seventy-five workers and the sheriff arrested about fifteen others.

The events of 1883 were soon followed by new labor actions in 1884, when the Iron Mountain attempted to reduce wages. In October, as a result of general economic problems throughout the region, Jay Gould's Southwestern railroad system cut wages 10 percent. The action affected hundreds of employees on the Iron Mountain branch of the Missouri Pacific line in Arkansas. In response, leaders of the railroad unions linked their locals with a national organization, the Knights of Labor. Local assemblies were formed in 1884, and even though the Arkansas Knights did not participate in the Southwestern strike, the national union's success in forcing the railroad to revoke the wage cut sparked a rapid growth for the movement. In 1885 the locals, consisting primarily of railroad men and confined for the most part to central Arkansas, formed a state assembly. Other assemblies developed quickly in the western coal mines as well as among some lumber workers.

Originally concerned with changing job conditions, the Knights in Arkansas were politicized by events in 1886. When the national organization of the Knights declared a general strike against Gould's Southwestern railroads in March of that year, the Arkansas Knights were ready. The call was prompted by labor problems in Texas, but the Arkansas union went out in support of the Texas Knights and also to ask for higher wages and to secure recognition for the union. The strike began quietly, but management efforts to operate freight trains anyway led to acts of violence in which workers disabled forty-five locomotives at the Iron Mountain's Baring Cross shops in Argenta (North Little Rock), destroyed other company property, and intimidated workers who remained on the jobs.

Local businessmen were initially sympathetic with the workers, but discovering that their own business was hurt as the 1886 strike dragged on, began to express opposition. Claiming that its continuation made the general public suffer for the good of the few, conservative interests placed more and more pressure on the workers to end their strike and put the railroads back into operation. On March 24, Governor Hughes directed the Iron Mountain to resume regular operations, although not clearly stating how the government would enforce this resumption of action. Of course the resumption of service without concessions from the railroad would be a defeat for labor. This is what happened as the strike ended when the Knights capitulated, unable to sustain public support, declaring that this was in the public interest. The result of their failure was that 95 percent of the striking workers lost their jobs.

The strike of 1886, plus the Haymarket Bombing in Chicago later that year, helped destroy the Knights of Labor nationally, but in Arkansas unionization continued and union leaders increasingly became interested in politics. After the role of the Democratic government in breaking the strike, many labor activists concluded that their success required political action and the defeat of the Democratic Party, which dominated the state. Even though their specific interests did not coincide, the desire to defeat the Democrats made the Knights and the politically active Wheel leaders potential allies. In the 1886 campaign season, members of the Knights of Labor met with the Pulaski County Wheel to discuss grounds for cooperation. They were unable to agree on a county ticket at that time, but a successful combination was not long in the future. Through the next year, Wheelers and union men continued to talk about the possibilities of cooperation.

Members of these groups advocating political action finally came together with the organization of the Union Labor Party in 1888. The new party held its first state convention at Little Rock on April 30 of that year. During four days of deliberation, the delegates produced a platform that brought together the goals of the Agricultural Wheel and the Knights, although it looked much like that adopted by the Wheel in 1886. They called for the usual economic reforms—a new monetary system and closer regulation of corporations. Once again they wanted the convict labor system abolished and limitations on the immigration of Chinese laborers. They advocated, however, an even larger role for government, seeking mine regulations, state control of trusts, a national system of education, and national and state bureaus of labor and agriculture. In a direct attack upon what they considered the entrenched Democratic Party, the delegates called for changes in the electoral process to eliminate fraud, which they considered the chief means the Democrats had used to maintain power.

To head their ticket in 1888, the delegates selected a one-legged Confederate veteran and former legislator from Prescott, C. M. Norwood. Representing a broadened coalition of farmers and laborers, Norwood's threat to the Democratic Party's nominee, James P. Eagle, grew when Arkansas Republicans threw Norwood their support. Norwood campaigned vigorously, touring the state and emphasizing the basic theme he had advanced when he accepted his nomination. He believed that all the forces of labor had finally come together in the new party and that it was time to "strike decisive blows for the emancipation of enslaved labor in the upcoming campaign." To him, government's first duty was to "protect, foster and encourage industry," but he believed that instead it was in the hands of hostile forces who produced laws "unjustly discriminating in favor of capital and capitalists, and withholding from the honest producer and laborer the full and just reward of their toil and sweat." He pointed particularly to the power of banks, railroads, and entrenched politicians, and promised to restrict their power in the community. He also promised vigorous support for education and for immigration to promote the state's development.

Norwood's optimism concerning the unity of labor was unrealistic. The Union Labor Party had problems from the beginning. Many Wheelers had never favored political action and were certainly hostile to the creation of a third party. Encouraged by Democratic leaders, many local Wheel groups bolted the state organization and returned their charters because of the organization's new political stance. These dissatisfied Wheelers, still convinced that some sort of organization was necessary, formed two rival groups: the Farmer's Cooperative Alliance of Arkansas and the Farmer's Alliance of Arkansas. Even for those Wheelers who might support political action, a strong tradition of hostility towards the Republican Party made the Union Labor organization unacceptable. Aware of the discontent and the actual withdrawal of some local Wheels from the state organization, leaders, even though many of them had helped to create the new party, backed away from a formal endorsement of the Union Labor ticket when they held their state convention in July.

The schism within the Wheel may have reduced farmer support for Union Labor, but the Democrats took the new party as a serious challenge. In the campaign that followed they used every means possible to fight Norwood and his party. Eagle's public campaign was based on an appeal to the issues that had maintained the Democratic majority since Redemption. The Democrats proclaimed themselves still the party of state's rights and opposed any interference in state or local affairs by the federal government, a position linking their party to the Confederate past and white supremacy. In addition, they pointed to their fiscal conservatism which had produced tax cuts and a solution to the state's debt problems, a stance that had long appealed to propertied interests.

Eagle's supporters were not content to let the issues speak for themselves, however, and Union Labor leaders charged that the Democrats used less savory means as well. Local campaigners played upon racial fears, charging that Norwood's election would produce a return to the days of Republican rule during Reconstruction. In some cases, Democrats used violence to intimidate voters and reduce turnout. Voting boxes were tampered with or disappeared. Union Labor leaders were convinced the ultimate fraud came when the vote was counted: the Democrats simply falsified returns and counted Norwood out.

Despite all that had been done, Norwood received significant support. The Union Labor candidate received 84,213 votes out of a total of 183,427 votes cast, about 46 percent throughout the state. Even though Norwood's challenge to the Democracy had failed, the fusion between the Union Labor and Republican Parties behind a single candidate posed a serious challenge to Democratic domination of state politics.

In many ways, the threat posed by Norwood to the Democratic Party's control over state government in 1888 set the scene for a partisan reaction that destroyed the possibilities for agrarian reform within the state. The willingness of farm leaders who supported Union Labor to link both with African-Americans and organized labor raised serious questions about Arkansas's political future. It potentially created a majority party based on a class interest —that of poorer Arkansans. Not only did such a coalition threaten Democratic control of the state government, it also posed a potential threat to the economic and social interests empowered by Democratic rule.

The 1888 election was followed by a continuing Democratic assault upon the political farmers. One of the party's strategies was to encourage the growth of alternative organizations that would draw support away from the Wheel. The group most supported by Democrats was the Farmer's Alliance.

The Farmer's Alliance was actually a national organization. In the spring of 1887 several local Alliances created the Farmer's Alliance of Arkansas, but the national leadership gave the state charter to the Wheel instead of this group. For a time local Alliances operated under the Wheel, but in the spring of 1888 groups opposing the Wheel's increasing politicization had broken away to form originally two different state organizations. In 1889 the Wheel surrendered the state Alliance charter, and the Farmer's Cooperative Alliance and Farmer's Alliance merged into a reorganized state Alliance that July.

At the meeting of the unified Alliance, leaders and delegates asserted their intention of making the organization apolitical. Their new president, W. S. Grant, emphasized the need to return to the principles of self-help and to abandon politics. The delegates resolved to revoke the charters and erase from the roll the names of any county or subordinate Alliance "who shall bring politics into their Alliances, or shall put out a ticket." The rabidly pro-Democrat *Arkansas Gazette* congratulated the Alliance men for their course, concluding, "We hope to see the Alliance boom in Arkansas." In effect, the Alliance offered a way of depoliticizing agrarian dissent within the state.

Alliance rhetoric was every bit as radical as that of the Wheel, but without the call for political action. Pres. W. S. Grant's annual address in 1889 declared the conflict engaged in by his group as "warfare." He saw a battle in which the "monopolists of the country, whose greed know no bounds, are constantly scheming to get from the producer, the artisan and laborer that which does not rightly belong to them." But for Grant and other leaders, resolution of the conflict would not come with independent political action. Instead it would come with the concerted action of all laboring men. "Co-operation," he said, "is the key that unlocks the future; co-operation in everything pertaining to our interests." Grant offered the farmer a vehicle of protest. The Alliance offered the Democratic Party no challenge.

State Democratic leaders also moved to undermine the agrarian threat by making more concessions to farm radicals in their own platform. The 1890 state platform, for example, drifted away from the party's traditional positions and made more of a class appeal. They called for free and unrestricted coinage of silver, a policy that would have inflated the nation's monetary supply and possibly would have reduced the cost of money by lowering interest rates and infusing more capital into the economy. The Democrats also endorsed a plank that called for the creation of a system to regulate the rates for railroad freight and passenger service. Though they did not offer as much reform as the Union Labor radicals, their platform did give voters something of a compromise. They offered relief and change, but within the structure of the traditional party apparatus.

At the same time, Democratic leaders sought to break up the racial coalition that had appeared so dangerous in 1888. Beginning the following year, Democratic newspapers encouraged the disfranchisement of blacks. They usually argued that this should be done to get rid of ignorant voters, but the effect would be to remove them as a potential ally of poor white farmers in challenging the Democratic Party's political dominance. Arguing that the government of Arkansas belong to the white man, most of the major newspapers demanded that the political power of African-Americans be eliminated.

By 1890 the Democrats had begun action that would undercut their challengers, but the overall strategy was not yet complete. Union Labor fielded more candidates to challenge Democrats running for many state offices. The Union Labor convention met at Little Rock on June 10. Their platform repeated that of 1888, calling for free and fair elections, government regulation of banking, government control over the monetary supply, and control over business monopolies. They nominated Napoleon B. Fizer of White County as their candidate for governor. The Republican Party, meeting at Glenwood on July 9, 1890, once again agreed to a fusion with Union Labor, endorsing Fizer because of his support of free and fair elections.

In the election, the Democrats renominated Governor Eagle on a platform embracing a number of reform measures, but once again violence and intimidation were used to ensure a Democratic victory. The election results suggested that the farm challenge may have peaked with this campaign. Fizer improved upon the vote of Norwood in 1888, receiving 85,181 votes, but Eagle polled an even greater number than in the previous election. The fusion candidate's proportion of the total popular vote slipped to 44 percent.

Despite the failure of Fizer to expand Union Labor's vote significantly, the number he received still represented a potentially dangerous threat, and Democrats continued their efforts to disable the farm movement. With action initiated in the Twenty-eighth Legislature in 1891, the Democratic majority completed efforts to destroy party fusion and to remove the threat of any sort of coalition of poor farmers by implementing an effective program of disfranchising black voters. As has been shown by historian John W. Graves, the ultimate destruction of fusion and black voting took place as a result of the state's election law of 1891. Under the guise of election reform, the general assembly passed a bill that did much to eliminate some of the worst forms of political corruption at the local level. On the other hand, the new law created a centralized election bureaucracy, taking control out of the hands of local authorities, and also provided that illiterates could vote only when precinct judges marked their tickets, establishing elaborate procedures for that process. Opponents concluded that the bill was intended to ensure that local election machinery did not fall into the hands of dissidents and to provide mechanisms that could be used to discourage the 13 percent of white and 56 percent of black voters who were illiterate at the time.

In the 1892 election, the results of the assembly's actions were apparent, although the race was vigorously contested. Agrarian protest continued, although in a much modified form. Nationally, the Farmer's Alliance had recognized the need to support an independent party and had helped to form the People's, or Populist, Party that year. In Arkansas, supporters of the Farm Labor Party reorganized and took the national name. For governor, the Populists nominated J. P. Carnahan. Their platform reflected the traditional agrarian reform program, although locally as well as nationally they placed increasing emphasis upon currency expansion, free coinage of silver, and a paper currency tied to the size of the population as the means to solve economic problems. Unlike the previous two elections, the Populists were unable to secure a fusion with the Republicans, who ran William G. Whipple. The votes of those opposed to the state's Democrats was further fragmented with the appearance of a new party, the Prohibition Party, which ran its own candidate, William J. Nelson. The Democrats nominated William M. Fishback.

In the election on September 5, officials enforced the new literacy law. At Hampton in Calhoun County some blacks went to the polls armed, determined to vote anyway, but were not allowed to do so. When they persisted, election officials resorted to violence. The end result, although newspapers called it a race war, was the massacre of at least four blacks and the arrest of others for disturbing the peace. Across the state, however, the Hampton example was not typical. Most blacks simply declined to go to the polls rather than deal with the election judges. A correspondent of the *Arkansas Gazette* reported that in Hempstead County, blacks who could not read or write refused to vote because they did not wish to undergo the process required. In Desha County, white Democrats believed that the new law had demoralized black voters and ensured their success. For the first time since black enfranchisement, the overall voter and black turnout was reduced, and total voter turnout dropped 18 percent, from 191,448 in 1890 to 156,192 in 1892. Fishback easily carried the election with 58 percent of the vote, the largest proportion received by a Democratic candidate after the outbreak of farm discontent.

Fishback's large percentage, however, was based on a decline in the number of voters. Disfranchisement worked well to remove men from the voting roles. Through the rest of the century, the dominant trend at elections was a decline in the number of voters. In fact, the number of voters did not surpass the 1890 gubernatorial election returns of 191,448 again until 194,292 citizens cast their votes in the 1924 Democratic primary. Even the 1924 election does not show fully the long-term effects of the disfranchising election laws, since by that year the potential electorate had been expanded with the addition of women voters. In that thirty-four-year period, the nadir was reached in the 1918 general election when only 72,984 voted.

The election laws probably decreased election participation among both races, but clearly the greatest impact was on black voters. Election statistics do not show participation by race, but the results showed the destruction of African-Americans as a political force in the state. As late as 1891, twelve black legislators still sat in the general assembly, eleven in the House of Representatives and one in the Senate. Many other local officials were African-Americans, particularly in the counties with large black populations. By 1893 all blacks had disappeared from the legislature, and they virtually vanished from local offices as well.

Disfranchisement did not bring an end to the farm protest movement, but it essentially ended any real chance for its success outside of the Democratic Party. Economic conditions through the 1890s provided fertile grounds for continued discontent among many Arkansans. From 1892 through 1900, the Populist Party offered candidates for governor. Republicans joined the Populists in 1894, but thereafter ran their own candidates. Neither the Populist-Republican fusion ticket nor the individual party tickets mounted a serious threat to the Democrats. From receiving 46 percent of the vote in 1888, Democratic opponents steadily slipped downward. By the turn of the century they could count on no more than about 30 percent of the vote in general elections.

With little chance to affect the direction of politics independently, many who had pushed for reform as supporters of the Farm Labor or Populist Parties moved back to the Democratic Party. There they were able to continue to play a political role. In fact, inside the Democratic Party a struggle was going on that potentially gave the agrarians more voice. From the end of Reconstruction, the Democrats had used policies of fiscal conservatism, limited government, and white supremacy to tie poor white farmers to a party that was dominated by the landowning interests of the state. To defeat Union Labor and the Populists, however, some leaders had pushed for party policy more favorable to the interests of the protesters. At the same time, they were willing to make even more overt appeals to the class and racial fears of white voters. For a short time, power within the Democratic Party shifted to these "agrarian" leaders.

James P. Clarke in 1894 and Daniel W. Jones in 1896 embraced this new agrarianism within the Democratic Party to secure the gubernatorial nomination and win the general election. Both advocated a movement away from the gold standard and a policy of "Free Silver." Silver, used as a basis for national currency and unlimitedly coined, promised an inflation of the amount of money in circulation that many farmers believed would bring down the cost of credit and the prices of goods they purchased. The candidates also were open to regulation of the railroads and other corporations. At the same time, both men made overt appeals to the racial fears of their constituents. Clarke asked for votes on the grounds that it was the Democratic Party that would maintain "white standards of civilization."

The legacy of demagoguery persisted into the twentieth century in the administration of Jeff Davis. Davis successfully appealed to lower class hostility to the state's elites and racial fears to gain the governor's office three times between 1900 and 1906. He campaigned on the idea that the ills confronted by Arkansans at the turn of the century were the result of, in the words of political scientist Calvin R. Ledbetter, "a national conspiracy." In collusion with the wealthy urbanites within Arkansas itself, Wall Street and trusts had moved to concentrate wealth at the expense of the people. Davis also appealed strongly to the state's racist tradition and to its Southern identity. He dramatically demonstrated his position by campaigning in a suit of Confederate gray. Davis's appeal, with its explicit condemnation of the power and lifestyles of the nation's powerful, secured him widespread rural support in election after election.

Davis's career in office, however, raised questions about the radicalism of this critical turn-of-the-century politician. As attorney general, he prosecuted trusts and as governor he introduced and secured in the legislature an anti-trust law. He also attacked what he considered the wasting of the poor man's taxes, pushing especially against the construction of the present state capitol. In addition, he attacked the convict-leasing system and pushed for changes in the state penitentiary system. Ultimately, however, none of these reforms seriously changed conditions within the state. On the whole, he did little to threaten the status quo.

Despite their personal successes between 1894 and 1906, Clarke, Jones, and Davis's administrations represented only a short interlude between the dominance of state government by the Conservative-Redeemer leaders from 1874 to 1894 and the emergence of a new type of leadership, the Progressives, by 1906. Even as these three men made their successful campaign appeals, new conditions developing in the state undermined their approaches to government. The economy, in fact, appeared to better itself. The move from the countryside to the town continued. Forces were unleashed that made an appeal to agrarian ideas less rewarding. Arkansans appeared on the verge of securing the "New Arkansas" they had hoped for since the end of Reconstruction.

Turn-of-the-Century
Prosperity and Challenges

Agricultural problems in the 1880s and early 1890s appeared to deflect the people of Arkansas from the economic change they had envisioned. That diversion turned out to be only a temporary one, however. From the mid-1890s into the first two decades of the twentieth century economic conditions improved. The editors of the *Arkansas Gazette* welcomed the New Year and the new century in 1900, concluding that after years of crisis and stagnation the future was one of promise. Everything in Arkansas, they believed, was headed in the right direction. While only a few years before the South had been depressed and its economy stagnant, the turning point had been reached and the entire region was making strides in the direction of "progress." The editors saw increased investments in manufacturing and improved markets as signals of a new era. As always, the *Gazette's* editors may have been too optimistic, but change was taking place. The forces that had produced so much hopefulness earlier continued to be active, and the state's integration into the national market proceeded at a faster pace. Continued economic development brought with it a variety of new problems, but coming out of an economic depression most of Arkansas's leaders preferred to avert their attention from these questions in their excitement about new prospects.

Between 1900 and 1920 a wide variety of impulses pushed the Arkansas economy forward, but the most important factor was the increase in demand for many goods produced in Arkansas. Prices rose steadily for agricultural, timber, mining, and manufacturing products from the end of the 1890s. Demand and rising prices were stimulated further by the outbreak of World War I, which forced many European nations to rely more heavily on American goods. Arkansans responded with increased productivity. New farm crops were introduced in response to market demand. Natural resources were developed further. Manufacturing advanced to the point that new, nationally competitive industries emerged.

Agriculture continued to be the dominant sector in the economy, but after a decade of hard times for farmers, the future looked much brighter. Having reached a low of 6 cents per pound in 1898, cotton prices began to climb. By 1900 it had reached 9.6 cents, ten years later it was at 15.1 cents. In 1917, the first year of the world war for Americans, cotton prices reached 23.5 cents, then peaked three years later at 33.9 cents. Corn prices, which had been at 28 cents in 1889, reached $1.52 per bushel in 1919. Wheat prices had bottomed out in 1894 at 55.9 cents per bushel, then also began a heady ascent to its peak of $2.46 in 1920.

The chief effect of rising farm prices was a rush to increase the number of acres in cultivation, usually for the production of cash crops. In the first decade of the century, nearly 36,000 new farms were started, bringing the total number of farms to 214,678 consisting of 17,416,075 acres. The rate of growth slowed during the next ten years, and farm acreage increased only moderately. Still, almost eighteen thousand new farmers started working during the 1910s.

Although long experience had shown Arkansas the problems of relying too heavily on a single crop, farmers plunged into cotton eagerly as prices rose. In 1900, 31.3 percent of land in cultivation was planted in cotton. By 1909 that proportion had increased to 40 percent. The war and good prices for other crops probably kept that percentage from going higher, but by 1919 farmers still had over 40 percent of their croplands in cotton. Despite cautions about such dependency, the payoff was enormous this time. The 1,641,855 bales harvested in 1899 had been worth about $217 million. The 1909 crop of 2,153,222 bales was only 31 percent larger but, bringing in $650 million, was twice as valuable. By 1919 the size of the crop had increased only a little, but the value had increased 166 percent to nearly $1.75 billion.

The farm picture improved not only because better prices produced a new prosperity in traditional farming communities but also because individual farms and some regions undertook significant diversification. One of the most important changes in commercial farming began at the turn of the century when increasing prices for rice and more secure markets encouraged some farmers to look to it as a replacement for cotton. As early as 1893 Paul Williams, a black farmer in Lonoke County, experimented with raising rice. Ultimately, however, it was William H. Fuller, a farmer from near Carlisle, who established rice cultivation as a successful venture in the state. Fuller visited Louisiana to learn about rice cultivation, then attempted to grow the crop on his farm, planting some three acres of land in rice in 1897. In 1904, after moving to Louisiana and actually engaging in the cultivation of rice, Fuller returned to Arkansas and planted seventy acres of rice and produced a first crop of 5,225 bushels, a yield of 75 bushels to the acre (and a good profit with rice selling at one dollar per bushel). Fuller later estimated that it had cost him $3,147 to put in the first crop, including sinking a well for irrigation.

Fuller's success produced a rice boom in Arkansas. As quickly as farmers were able to clear it, thousands of acres of land, bounded by the Missouri border on the north, the Arkansas River on the south, the St. Francis River on the east, and the Cache River on the west, were either converted from cotton production to rice cultivation or originally opened in the first decades of the twentieth century. By 1909 the state had become the third most important rice producer in the nation with the harvesting of 1,282,830 bushels. In 1919 the state's farms were second in the nation, producing 6,797,126 bushels. Although its value could not match the importance of cotton statewide, rice represented an enormous part of the economic life in the counties producing the new crop.

In addition to the introduction of rice, fruit and truck farming also continued to attract attention. At least in part, this development was encouraged by the further expansion of the railroads into previously undeveloped markets. The completion of the Missouri and North Arkansas between Eureka Springs and Helena in 1909 was of particular importance, providing market access to orchard growers in Carroll, Boone, Searcy, Van Buren, and Cleburne Counties. While the cultivation of many berries remained relatively unchanged, the apple harvest tripled between 1899 and 1919, and the peach harvest increased over 900 percent during the same time. The number of acres planted in tomatoes, snap beans, peas, and cantaloupes also multiplied throughout the state along the rail lines.

The timber industry continued the expansion it had begun in the 1880s and 1890s. Despite the significant cutting that had taken place before the turn of the century, the state's forests were still extensive. The timber companies, usually waiting for railroad access, moved into new lands as quickly as development was feasible. For example, the Memphis, Helena, and Louisiana Railroad, ultimately to become a part of the Missouri Pacific system, encouraged expanded timber operations in southeastern Arkansas. Where the railroad went, prices for good timberlands skyrocketed. Near Dumas, two-dollar land jumped to fifteen dollars an acre with the arrival of the Memphis, Helena, and Louisiana.

The most important development of new timberlands, however, was the opening of the 6,000 square miles of "Sunk Lands" along the St. Francis River in Craighead, Mississippi, and Poinsett Counties. The Sunk Lands had been created by the New Madrid earthquakes of 1811–1812 and were subject to overflows from the Mississippi River. These were potentially some of the richest lands in the state, and during the 1890s access was improved with the construction of levees and a drainage system. In 1897 businessmen at Jonesboro began building the Jonesboro, Lake City, and Eastern Railroad. The road went from near Jonesboro, to Lake City, then north and east to Monette, Leachville, and Blytheville. Cutting through the heart of the area, the line opened up the Sunk Lands for extensive development by timber companies and prospered.

The industry benefited as well from increasing demand for its products. General economic activity accounted in part for this increase, but after 1914 the war in Europe also played a role. In 1915 sawmills at Helena and Brasfield received orders for 25,000,000 feet of walnut to be milled into gunstocks at Memphis. Another company that received an order for wood to be used by an arms manufacturer pointed out that, as a result of this, their mills would be working at capacity for a full year. Few lumber yards would have enjoyed such productivity in previous years.

Timber cutting continued apace as new lands opened and new opportunities appeared. In 1899 there had been 1,199 establishments engaged in the cutting and rough processing of timber. By 1909 that number had increased to 1,697 mills. The amount of wood being processed also grew, expanding at a rate of 30 percent between 1899 and 1909, from 1,623,987 to 2,111,300 board feet. Production softened by 1919, however, and the 1920 census reported that only 1,506 companies were still engaged in the timber industry, and production had dropped to 1,772,157 board feet.

The problem with the timber industry was that it was quickly exhausting the state's forests. As the techniques of cutting trees became more efficient, companies could remove large quantities of virgin forests quickly. Developers estimated that the new timberlands of the northeastern counties of the state would hardly last beyond fifteen or twenty years. It took even less time than that, and the days of easy logging were disappearing quickly as new stands of virgin timber became increasingly difficult to find.

The utilization of other natural resources in the state at the turn of the century also increased at a rapid pace. Throughout the period, coal mining remained the most important extractive industry, both in terms of its work force and the value of its product. In 1900 some thirty-three companies operated fifty-three mines and employed 2,574 workers. They produced 1,943,932 tons of coal, valued at $2,539,214. By 1919 the census listed some eighty-five "enterprises" engaged in mining, although the number of workers had increased to only 2,787. The value of the product, however, had risen dramatically to $5,292,274.

Even though the long-term statistics indicated prosperity in the coal fields, difficulties existed. Periodic labor problems caused some companies to discontinue mining operations in the state, at least until the outbreak of war increased prices. Productivity actually declined at various times before the war. Reflecting these problems, in December 1915 one of the oldest coal mines in the state (at Jenny Lind) was abandoned.

Economic activity in the extractive industries received a further boost from increasing demand for petroleum products. A variety of innovations, particularly the production of automobiles, made oil an increasingly important commodity, and prices rose steadily after 1900. Discoveries of large oil and gas fields throughout the Southwest encouraged exploration and development in Arkansas, especially in western Arkansas, where known deposits of natural gas existed. However, through the 1900s and 1910s industrialists found very little oil, but continuing discoveries of gas convinced them that oil was present. Although rooted in the first two decades of the century, the petroleum industry would not fully emerge until 1920, when significant oil deposits were found in Ouachita and Union Counties—the edges of the El Dorado Pool. By 1921 some five hundred wells had been dug near El Dorado, producing more than ten million barrels of oil. Moving out from the El Dorado Pool, drillers found additional deposits, including the Irma Pool in Nevada County and the Smackover Pool near El Dorado. In 1922 some nine hundred wells were drilled in Arkansas. Tens of thousands of barrels of oil a day poured from the ground.

In addition to exploration and development, processing and refining of petroleum products were parts of the industry in southern Arkansas. By August 1921 five refineries were in operation at El Dorado. Among the most successful of these was Lion Oil and Refinery, organized by local citizens in 1922 but ultimately taken over by outside owners. Lion steadily expanded through the 1920s from refining crude oil brought in from nearby fields to a major national oil company involved in research, exploration, transportation, and retail marketing.

Rising prices, plus the outbreak of the world war, were particularly important in the development of new industries mining other mineral resources in the state. Bauxite, the ore from which aluminum is extracted, was the most significant of these, with deposits located primarily southwest of Little Rock in Saline County. In 1896 the General Bauxite Company opened the first working mine in the bauxite fields. The deposits proved rich enough that other companies also moved in, including the Pittsburgh Reduction Company, forerunner to Alcoa Aluminum. Pittsburgh Reduction, owned by Andrew Mellon, began buying lands in 1899, and in 1905 established effective control over bauxite mining by acquiring General Bauxite.

The Arkansas mines developed slowly. At the beginning there were problems moving the ore to processing facilities, making ore from the Arkansas fields too expensive. Operations expanded, however, when World War I broke out. French sources of bauxite were cut off, and military use of aluminum in a variety of products from shell fuses to motor parts raised prices. As a result, Alcoa, the only major producer of aluminum in the country, expanded its production and further developed the Arkansas fields. Between 1915 and 1917 aluminum production within the country increased nearly 50 percent, with Arkansas mines supplying most of the raw materials necessary. Equipment was modernized and employment increased—by 1917 the mines employed over two thousand workers.

Bauxite was not the only extractive industry that expanded as a result of higher prices generated by wartime demand. By 1915 many European mines and smelters had closed and American zinc prices had doubled, rising from $50 per ton to a record high of $100 per ton. Zinc deposits had always been known to exist in northwestern Arkansas, and small mine operations had been in place throughout the late nineteenth century. Higher prices encouraged increased exploration and mining both in the Missouri and Arkansas Ozarks. Newton, Marion, and Boone Counties saw a proliferation of lead and zinc mines and heavier investment in actual mining efforts.

As in the case of bauxite, zinc production in Arkansas was largely restricted to the simple extraction of the ore. Developers theorized that electric smelters might be efficiently constructed in the mountains, using the region's rivers to generate hydroelectric power. For whatever reason, none of these schemes ever developed. As a result, the industry remained focused around mining. Local miners carried their ore by wagon to the town of Harrison, which became a major shipping center for transporting zinc to other sites for processing.

In addition to improvements in agriculture and mining, the state's manufacturing sector also boomed following the turn of the century. With census figures adjusted to remove those businesses associated with lumber, the state had 547 companies engaged in manufacturing pursuits in 1899. By 1909 that number had increased 124 percent to 1,228. In the next decade the increase was 32 percent to 1,617 establishments. The value of products, however, grew at an even faster rate. In the first decade of the century the value of manufactured goods increased 115 percent from $15,927,595 to $34,276,040; by 1920 this figure had grown 239 percent to $116,304,549.

As in the nineteenth century, industries connected to timber and those that processed agricultural goods continued to be the most important in Arkansas. The cottonseed oil and cake industry was the most valuable, with an annual product worth $25,304,034 in 1919—nearly 22 percent of the total value of the state's manufactured goods. Taken together, the companies that made finished-wood items—turned and carved woods, planing mill products, barrels, and furniture—accounted for nearly 9 percent of the total manufacturing of the state. Good economic times encouraged this growth, and the war generated even greater demands as local mills manufactured everything from gunstocks to oars.

In the larger towns, more sophisticated industries continued to develop. Railroad shops at Pine Bluff and Little Rock repaired rolling stock and equipment and actually built cars. These employed more workers than any other single industry. Larger towns also had increasingly diversified economies. At Little Rock, in addition to the usual activities, factories made foundry and machine-shop products, mattresses and spring beds, artificial limbs, baskets, carriages and wagons, clothing, dental products, furniture, and even automobiles. At Fort Smith the manufacture of furniture, refrigerators, carriages, and wagons made it in many ways similar to contemporary northern industrial towns.

Of all these businesses, the appearance of automobile manufacturing at Little Rock held the most promise for breaking from the state's agrarian tradition. In 1919 three Little Rock businessmen organized the Climber Motor Corporation, capitalized at one million dollars, hoping to produce inexpensive cars that could underprice Detroit products and better stand conditions on Southern roads. At a rate of two a day by 1920, Climber was producing cars for the South, which "demands a sturdier and stronger built car than any other part of the United States, and it is with a full understanding of the needs and uses of the people of the South that this car is designed and manufactured." The Climber Corporation was a symbol of the peak of industrial development in the state. Its very existence suggested that a New Arkansas had arrived and marked the culmination of twenty years of growth.

The overall economic picture for Arkansas after 1900 was bright. Farmers as a whole experienced a prosperity greater than that of any time since before the Civil War. Other industries matched or outpaced agricultural expansion. The steady rise in wages indicated this progress. Between 1900 and 1920 the income of salaried employees—white-collar workers—in manufacturing increased from $758 per year to $2,043. Wage laborers also benefited. Average salaries for those in manufacturing increased from $327 to $944 annually in that same period. In the mining industry, wages increased from $564 to $1,259 per year.

Within the framework of prosperity and expanding economic opportunities two major social trends continued. First, although Arkansas remained primarily a rural state, more and more of its people moved to cities. Second, while the new conditions made it possible for urban people to increase their material possessions and make life even more comfortable, a larger number of rural people were able to share a part of the urban lifestyle. It appeared that all of the state was being integrated into a common economy and culture.

The census pointed clearly to the urban trend. Arkansas remained a predominantly rural state, but the urban population was steadily growing. From only 8.5 percent of all Arkansas residents in 1900, the urban population increased to 12.9 percent in 1910 and then to 16.6 percent by 1920. In the latter year, Little Rock had 65,142 inhabitants, Fort Smith 28,870, Pine Bluff 19,280, and Hot Springs 11,695. That same year the census listed twenty-six other incorporated cities and 320 incorporated towns. No matter how small, each was tied into the thriving economy and its citizens aspired to become the new commercial center of their county, if not the state.

The expansion of manufacturing was particularly important in the growth of older towns, but the continuing movement of railroads was central to the emergence and growth of new ones. The fate of Harrison, along the line of the Missouri and North Arkansas, was typical. With access to markets, new industries involved in the processing and marketing of locally produced goods boomed. Canning factories for fruits as well as saw-mills and woodworking facilities—including stave mills, broom handle factories, hub and spoke mills, cooperage plants, box factories, and veneer plants—all appeared. Across the state, new towns like DeQueen, Dierks, Gillett, Huttig, Horatio, Leslie, and McGehee appeared along railroad lines and as centers of commerce or new industries within their surrounding regions. The impact of a single road was exemplified by the Missouri and North Arkansas: when completed, thirty-three new towns had been created along its route.

The wealth generated by the prosperity of the early twentieth century contributed greatly to the second major trend—an integration of the people of the state into the national market and culture. Among urban inhabitants, newspaper advertisements indicated the availability of more and more goods that were produced throughout the nation, suggesting the increasing material comfort of these Arkansans. By 1910 the *Arkansas Gazette* offered Little Rock buyers a wide variety of merchandise manufactured elsewhere and shipped into the state. Cans of Carnation Brand Sterilized Evaporated Cream could be bought at C. J. Kramer & Co., a brass bed for only $16.50 at Jones Housefurnishing Co., an Apollo Player Piano at Hollenberg Music Co., and a 1911 Overland two-passenger business runabout for $775 from Tedford Auto. The housewife looking for labor-saving devices could buy a General Electric motor to attach to her sewing machine at Electric Construction Co. or a gas range—"the cleanest, most economical, quickest, and most convenient way to cook"—from the Pulaski Gas Light Co. If nothing else, someone looking for a deal could get a free six-quart steel enameled mixing bowl when they purchased fifty cents worth of products at the Great Atlantic and Pacific Tea Co., the A&P, on Main Street.

The growing availability of new products was not confined to the city. Rural folks had access to larger numbers of goods that could be considered luxuries, and they probably bought them. At Rogers, in the middle of the northwestern farming country, B. W. Quisenberry's Pharmacy in 1907 offered Kodak cameras and supplies for the expert or amateur photographer, plus Spaulding sporting goods for the local baseball player. The Rogers Big Racket Store advertised the "latest and newest novelties direct from the Eastern markets" that same year. If nearby local merchants did not offer what the rural consumer wanted, the introduction of Rural Free Delivery at the turn of the century and parcel post service in 1913 allowed farmers to buy directly from Sears, Roebuck, and Company; Montgomery Ward; E. Butterick; or any number of mail order companies in Chicago and New York.

Improved economic circumstances did not just allow rural peoples to have more possessions, but also made it possible for them to become closer to the world around them. Expansion of postal service not only furthered the mail-order business, but also contributed to the general integration of rural neighborhoods into broader state and national communities. In the first decades of the new century, even rural families had access to state newspapers and national magazines that were common items in urban homes in the 1880s and 1890s. In addition, many farmers were also able to put in telephones as their financial circumstances made that expense possible. Telephones tied the rural household directly to the towns and to the entire state with the expansion of long-distance service.

Even rural social patterns changed. Country families, at least those who shared in the prosperity, were able to adopt a lifestyle that more closely mimicked that of their urban neighbors. Across the state, farm wives increasingly left the fields to take on the specialized household roles of the urban classes. Women became housekeepers and, to a greater degree, the parent charged with raising children. Even the lives of children changed, as it was possible for some to stay out of the fields longer, enjoy an extended childhood of play and education, and perhaps even aspire to leaving the farm altogether with the help of that schooling.

In many ways the United States's entry into World War I in 1917 furthered this integration of Arkansans into a national culture just as it had influenced the state's economy. The war brought many newcomers into the state. Camp Pike, an army training center, was located in North Little Rock, where recruits and draftees from Alabama, Louisiana, and Mississippi (as well as Arkansas) were organized into the Eighty-Seventh Division and where thousands of replacement troops who had joined the army from throughout the United States were subsequently trained. At Camp Eberts in Lonoke County, aviation students were trained to fly for the army. Contact with so many outsiders necessarily broadened the cultural view of the Arkansans around them.

For over seventy-one thousand Arkansans who served in the armed services, the war meant leaving the state and coming into contact with people from throughout the nation, as well as with people overseas. Little is known about the experiences of these men, but their service did introduce them quickly to the broader national culture, especially as it existed within the army. The Spanish-American War (1898) had been an important step toward reintegrating the South back into the Union. However, the large number of Southern men who served during World War I were more effectively nationalized, as were Arkansans, who now saw themselves as standing alongside the rest of their nation in opposing what they considered to be German aggression in Europe.

At home, participation in a variety of national organizations designed to provide support for the war effort brought other Arkansans into contact with the larger national culture. The state's Council of National Defense was responsible for war propaganda, administered the government's numerous programs designed to ensure enough supplies could be obtained by the national armies, and helped finance the war through the sale of war bonds. The Red Cross raised money to support its own efforts among the soldiers, and the YMCA not only raised money locally but also worked among the soldiers training in Arkansas. For those involved, the war years tied Arkansas closely to the nation, and many took pride in the part their state played in this national effort. They saw themselves not so much as second-class citizens but as full members of the nation.

The first two decades of the twentieth century clearly were golden years for many white Arkansans. The pervasiveness of the belief that the state finally was on the right track and was about to become a part of the rest of the nation in terms of prosperity and lifestyle had a strong basis in the reality of the situation. At the same time, there were problems. In agriculture and industry, the prosperity was not always shared equally, a fact that produced heightened tensions within communities. In addition, economic advancement created challenges to the status quo, especially to the longstanding patterns of race relations.

For individual farmers, changing circumstances often stood in the way of their sharing the good times caused by rising commodity prices. Many found themselves relegated to unprofitable holdings as the basic trend toward smaller and smaller farms continued. The problem was simple: despite some expansion of acreage in cultivation after the turn of the century, much of the arable land of the state had been opened by 1910, and yet the farm population continued to grow. This pressure on a fixed resource meant that the land was cut up into smaller and smaller pieces. The average farm size dropped from ninety-three acres in 1900 to eighty-one acres by 1910, then to seventy-five acres by 1920. The smallest units were inefficient, financially unable to use machinery, fertilizers, or pesticides, and the family typically struggled to survive.

The problem was compounded by the fact that to get to the land, many new farmers were forced to buy their farms on credit or to work as tenants rather than to cultivate land they owned outright. Mortgages suggest the use of credit for purchasing land, and the number of owner-operated farms with mortgages increased. In 1900 only 13.6 of owner-operated farms had mortgages, by 1910 that was 21 percent, then by 1920 it had risen to 30.2 percent. In addition, by 1910, 50 percent of farms were cultivated by tenants rather than owners, a figure that held in 1920. As in the late nineteenth century, the burden of interest payments, higher prices for supplies, and difficulties in marketing continued to limit the profits of the indebted farmers, even in good times.

By 1920 Arkansas basically had too many people trying to farm. The surplus population had only very limited avenues to escape from this situation, however. Relatively speaking, the revolution that was taking place in other local industries was remarkable, but the absolute number of new jobs that were being created at Little Rock, Pine Bluff, or Fort Smith were not enough to absorb the excess rural population. Even if the jobs had existed, inadequate education ill-suited many for the better manufacturing jobs, and a decade of agricultural depression had left others without the financial resources to even try to make it off the farm. The result was an increasing competition, practically a struggle, among farmers for available lands. In fact, rising prices made the fight among them even greater as individuals sought even more land in order to take advantage of the opportunity.

A major product of this struggle for land was heightened racial tension. In many areas, white tenants who wanted to expand the amount of land they were cultivating had to compete directly with black tenants for farmsteads. Rather than offering better bargains to landowners for their services, they often attempted to get rid of their competition by driving off blacks. For example, at the beginning of the contract season in January 1905, black tenants along the Lonoke-Jefferson County line were warned by a group known as the "Lonoke County Club" to vacate their farms because "This is a white man country for 1905." Planters and landowners blamed the threat on poor whites, who probably were responsible. Such episodes recurred throughout the era. Similar threats of violence occurred that April when a fruit farm at Horatio employed seventeen Mexican workers. Unknown parties tacked warnings on the Mexicans' cabin doors demanding that they leave and threatening violence if they did not.

While whites placed considerable pressure on blacks to keep their place, black farmers and tenants actually demonstrated a new resistance to the system that had kept them down economically for so long. Even though their actions often met with severe retaliation on the part of whites, black farm workers and tenants increasingly protested bad treatment by landowners. At Hope in January 1905, a dispute over money between two young black men and a white farmer led to a confrontation in which the latter was shot. One of the young blacks who had been involved in the fight was taken by a mob from a police officer who had arrested him and hanged. A labor dispute in March of the same year near Dumas between two blacks and a white planter led to the death of the planter; only the escape of the farm hands into a nearby swamp prevented their lynching.

The most serious confrontations came in eastern Arkansas, where organized labor was attempting to take advantage of discontent to develop a farmers' union. As early as 1915, organizers for the International Workers of the World, the Wobblies, attempted to organize black tenants and laborers in the cotton and rice fields. At least one local union was created, Robert Lee Hill's Progressive Farmers and Household Union of America, founded at Winchester in 1918 and modeled after the Negro Business League of Booker T. Washington. These efforts were strongly opposed by local landowners and businessmen, who feared the disruption of agriculture as a result. At Stuttgart, enraged whites tarred and feathered Wobblie organizers in 1917. Even Charles H. Brough, one of the state's more progressive governors, was hostile to the IWW and its efforts among farmers.

The attempt to create farm unions provided the framework for the state's most famous race riot—the Elaine Riot of October 1–14, 1919. The incident has never been explained fully and continues to provoke conflicting historical interpretations. It is clear that there was considerable discontent among black tenant farmers in 1918 and 1919. Objecting to the bookkeeping of local white landowners and charging them with cheating in order to keep the tenants in perpetual debt, blacks retaliated. They formed chapters of the PFHUA in the spring and summer of 1919 and hired lawyers to take legal action against the landowners under federal peonage statutes.

The validity of the tenant charges is unknown, but they were not improbable. Already tenants in Ashley and Lincoln Counties had won cases against planters who had sent county sheriffs after absent debtor tenants and then compelled them to work. The Phillips County tenants certainly believed they were being cheated, and in the summer of 1919 union members planned to withhold their cotton from market, determined to receive higher settlements. Believing that they would not be protected by the law, blacks decided to protect their own and began arming themselves.

For blacks to take up weapons against white landowners was too much for white communities to accept. Whites were certain that these plans amounted to a plot to rise up and kill local planters, to start some sort of insurrection. When gunfire broke out between union members and a Phillips County deputy sheriff and a police agent of the Missouri Pacific Railroad during a union meeting at a black church at Hoop Spur, whites were convinced the uprising had begun. The county sheriff organized a posse to arrest any troublemakers.

Blacks claimed that whites had fired into their meeting on September 30, but the posse moved in and began searching for union leaders, arresting both men and women. Blacks resisted with force, leading Governor Brough to send five hundred federal troops from Camp Pike near Little Rock to assist the posse. In the following days an unknown number of blacks were killed. Estimates put the number at between twenty-five and one hundred, but it is possible that many more were killed in the swamps along the Mississippi River in the southern part of the county. Hundreds were arrested. Five whites died during the riot.

The aftermath of the incident said much about race relations within the state. The governor appointed a special committee to investigate the incident. The committee consisted of prominent white citizens of Phillips County, including two plantation owners. They found that blacks had conspired to cause an insurrection and blamed them and outside agitators for what had happened, although investigators sent by the National Association for the Advancement of Colored People found no basis for such a conclusion. Ultimately, sixty-five of those arrested were tried for murder, eleven were found guilty and sentenced to death, the rest were sent to prison. National feeling that these blacks had been sentenced unjustly tied up the cases in court appeals, with the result that none were executed and those sentenced to death were ultimately released. The union, however, disintegrated.

Racial tensions were not confined to rural areas. Struggles over jobs in industries also often broke down along racial lines. Given their racist assumptions, whites in the towns usually considered it their right to have jobs before blacks got them. Some went so far as to drive potential black workers out of communities, thus securing their own positions. For example, at Des Arc on January 1915, when local mills that produced wood veneer began to lay off workers, notices appeared in public places demanding that black employees give up their jobs, adding an implicit threat to deal violently with those who refused.

In addition to race troubles, labor problems in the new industries were part of the era. In the extractive industries and manufacturing, increasing wages would suggest that this would have been a time of good labor relations, but pay rates often failed to tell the whole story. Among the greatest tensions was how management responded to changing market demand. In many cases, companies that had overproduced simply shut down their mills or plants until their surplus product had been sold and demand began to rise. In such situations workers were laid off. At other times, companies tried to cut pay for their workers in order to get through the slow times. No industry was immune to this situation. Even in the Little Rock and Pine Bluff railroad shops, where relatively stable work could be expected, this problem existed. Though hourly wages might look good, the lack of full annual employment allowed few workers to feel secure.

The general lack of company policies to provide any benefits for sick or injured workers added to this sense of insecurity. A laborer not present for work was not paid and was usually fired if off the job for any length of time. There were some exceptions. The Alcoa company created an Aid and Benefit System in which it matched voluntary employee contributions to a relief fund used to provide financial assistance to workers. However, few employees in the state had such a resource to fall back on.

Laborers had other complaints as well. Particularly in the timber and mining industries, where operations took place away from population centers that could provide adequate facilities, companies built "towns" or camps of some sort for their workers, providing housing, food, and entertainment. In some cases this reflected a practical and benevolent position by the employer. Alcoa's predecessor, the Pittsburgh Reduction Company, organized and ran the town of Bauxite because its managers believed employees would work better if they were properly housed, provided for in sickness and old age, given educational opportunities, and encouraged in communal cooperation. Other companies, however, used company facilities much as the landowner used the plantation store. Charging high prices for room and board and subtracting the totals from a worker's wages, the system had within it potential for abuse.

The persistent problems faced by labor meant that unions continued to exist in Arkansas, surviving the demise of the agrarian movement of the 1890s. The unions changed, however. Rather than focusing on broad-based social reforms, they placed greater emphasis upon specific grievances, particularly issues of pay, job security, and working conditions. Rather than political action, they turned almost exclusively to strikes to secure their specific goals. These strikes, always potentially violent given management's efforts to break them, added to the uneasiness that lay underneath the prosperity of the period.

In no industry was unrest more pervasive than in coal mining. The Knights of Labor had been successful in organizing coal miners in western Arkansas in the 1890s and had become part of the United Mine Workers by 1892–1893. As a part of the UMW, Arkansas miners received the same contracts as elsewhere in the nation, establishing pay rates that were considerably above the rates for most workers in the state. Mining companies from 1892 into the new century tried to break the UMW within the state and bring wages down to the level that could have been paid if there had been no national contract. As a result, strikes were frequent as workers tried to keep wages up and protect the union.

The most significant conflict took place in 1914, when one of the major coal mine operators in Arkansas, Franklin Bache (along with his partner Heber Denman), decided to break the control of the UMW by operating his mines as open shops. The miners accused Bache of seeking to make profits by paying lower wages, getting more work from his employees, and cutting the number of safety devices from his mines. On April 4, 1914, supported by private police from the W. J. Burns Detective Agency, Bache opened Mine No. 4 of the Prairie Creek Coal Mining Company in Sebastian County to nonunion labor.

On April 6, following the gathering of a large crowd of miners and their supporters at the Prairie Creek schoolhouse, three negotiators attempted to secure an agreement with the mine's superintendent to close the site. A conflict developed between the crowd and guards, however, and the mobs swarmed over barriers set around the mine, beat up the guards, and doused the fires under the mine's boilers. This last act made the mines temporarily unworkable, since water rose rapidly within the shafts until the pumps could be put back into operation. One miner carried a United States flag to the top of a tipple at the mouth of the mine and hung a fourteen foot banner that proclaimed: "This is Union Man's Country."

The owners refused to be cowed, however, and secured a restraining order against union members in the operation of the mine. While lawyers for both sides began their work in court, the UMW decided on April 20 to strike other mines worked by Bache in the area, beginning with the Coronado Coal Company site near Midland. Conditions continued to worsen, however, as the courts failed to secure any solution. The Bache companies began to bring in weapons in April. Union miners also began to arm by June. The conflict ultimately broke out on the night of July 17, when two hundred miners fought with company guards, killing two of the guards and destroying the mine. In the next several days mines were burned and dynamited elsewhere in the district.

The destruction of July 17, 1914, brought the Bache-Denman mines to a halt in western Arkansas, but short of preventing the opening of nonunion mines, little was accomplished by the workers. The sites remained closed, and the issues between owners and workers moved to the courts, where ultimately appeal after appeal brought the case to a stalemated conclusion. What was perhaps more critical, however, was how Arkansans viewed what was taking place in the western mines. Supported locally by people who depended on the miners for their own livelihood, there was little backing of the strikers elsewhere in the state.

Labor-management relations in other industries were also tense at times. Railroad workers in the American Railway Union periodically engaged in strikes. In one against the Pullman Palace Car Company in 1894, union members refused to handle Pullman cars and ultimately struck the railroads that insisted they do so. When the companies used strikebreakers, the union turned violent, destroying property at Little Rock and Pine Bluff. The strike was broken, however, when Gov. William M. Fishback sent the state militia into the railyards to protect railroad property and the federal government sent in United States marshals to ensure the delivery of the mail.

Even in the bauxite fields relationships were not always good. Despite the company's paternalistic policies, workers struck Pittsburgh Reduction in 1915 criticizing its wage policies and working conditions. When the company threatened to use force to break the strike, the workers backed down.

For Arkansans as a whole, the very presence of unions added to the tension that marked the changing economic world. While the conservative leadership of Arkansas sympathized with labor problems at times, generally they saw efforts at organization as potentially disruptive and threatening to produce unwanted change. Many nonunion Arkansans saw what was taking place as somehow vaguely un-American. Newspaper editors frequently criticized strikers, especially when their actions involved violence, accusing them of being anarchists. They blamed these actions on the large number of ignorant foreigners that they believed had filled up some of the unions and explained their actions as a failure to understand American civilization.

By 1920 many Arkansans who could remember the years before the twentieth century must have recognized the remarkable changes they had seen. The state had experienced considerable growth; its people had achieved a prosperity greater than at anytime since before the Civil War. Yet, that change had brought with it the breakdown of old ways. The availability of new consumer products and alterations in work produced new types of families. New industries brought unions and strikes. Race relations seemed more violent than ever. These conditions shattered what seemed to be the relatively clear lines that had defined the rural world and seemed to undermine any distinct sense of what order should be. Arkansans, in addition to everything else, were forced to search for some common identity and purpose.

They found this to be an almost impossible task. Issues of public morality were the clearest points where the breakdown of social and cultural unity could be seen; trying to define what was correct and moral only led to further struggle. When ministers tried to enforce traditional blue laws and close movie theaters on Sundays, they ran into vigorous opposition from owners, patrons, and even unions, which demanded that their members, who worked six days a week, have access to this form of entertainment. Efforts at closing saloons ran into protests from owners, patrons, and businessmen who thought of the establishments as another means of attracting consumers to town. A clear consensus on behavior had broken down.

The ability of religion to maintain unity in a community, a task already undermined by the multiplying of religious denominations, was weakened further by divisions within the denominations themselves. Trying to explain the diversity of the religious ideas they confronted and the heterogeneity of their world, some ministers and congregations struggled with new theology. Finis E. Maddox, a Presbyterian minister in Texarkana, probably reflected opinions in other denominations when he concluded that the Bible contained God's word, but only as interpreted by his people. It and religion were, thus, "broken echoes of the true," not absolute truth, and churches had to see direction in sense and reason. For others, such beliefs were heresy. Maddox was convicted of such charges by his own church in 1908. However, the idea that there was no single fundamental truth that could guide a community or apply to all circumstances survived, and the increasing conflict between this belief and others marked the collapse of religious authority.

Ultimately, however, for communities to exist they needed some sense of purpose, some means of organizing and ordering them. The social disarray apparent at the beginning of the twentieth century, plus the new prosperity that increasingly integrated all Arkansans into a broader world, provided the framework within which the people of the state turned more and more to government to provide the order they sought. In doing so, they adopted a mode of government already emerging in the city, one increasingly in the hands of specialists who sought reasoned or scientific solutions to problems. Along with people across the country, Arkansans advanced a revolution in government; they embraced political Progressivism.

The Progressive Years

The economic and social changes that were taking place, especially after the turn of the century, provided a framework within which a revolution in government took place in Arkansas. Building on a legacy of increasing public activity that had been present through the latter part of the nineteenth century, political leaders radically changed state government. These men and women began to understand how it could play a greater role in securing economic and social improvements—in achieving the promise of the New South in Arkansas. While problems remained that always limited their accomplishments, Arkansas's leaders proved remarkably innovative and farsighted in building a new state government.

These new ideas about state responsibilities paralleled similar developments at the national level. That new view of government and its role was called Progressivism. At the national level, this movement involved a new social and political philosophy that rejected a laissez-faire approach and advocated increasing centralization of power in the hands of a strong government. This was essential to Progressives because government had a new role to play in the increasingly complex urban-industrial society. Specifically, this role included regulating economic activity in ways to protect citizens from abuses, safeguarding the morality of the people, defending those who could not protect themselves, and planning for the future of the nation. Progressivism aimed at ending political corruption and evil; it sought efficiency and responsiveness to the people on the part of government. With America's economy and society changed, the role of government also had to change.

The Progressive belief that all of these things could be accomplished was based on new assumptions about the nature of human society and about the ability of people to solve their problems. These ideas were distinctly middle class in origin. Underlying their political philosophy was the belief that people were capable of understanding society through reason, through the same analytical processes that science had applied to nature. If causes were understood, conditions could be ameliorated and people and society put on a new course. Invariably, the Progressives believed that government must take the lead and provide agencies staffed by experts and technicians that could pinpoint problems and devise efficient solutions. If it did, the course of history could be changed.

The emergence of Arkansas Progressivism exhibited characteristics similar to those present on the national scene. Concern with ordering society had already pushed state government toward a greater economic and social role in the community during the nineteenth century. Continuing change as the century ended simply added to the strength of the forces demanding that government move ever faster in taking on its new role.

The sources for these reform ideas were present statewide. The idea of regulating businesses and industries that provided essential services to the state had been an important part of both the Farm Labor and Populist Party platforms during the late 1880s and 1890s. The state Socialist Party, receiving its support largely from western mine workers and union men in the towns, also encouraged a variety of reforms. Running its first gubernatorial candidate in 1904, the Socialists wanted state ownership of utilities and transportation, plus government programs for education, health insurance, and an old-age pension. The firmest footing for reform, however, was in the people of the towns and cities. Business associations, professional groups, women's organizations, societies advocating specific reforms, and even churches provided support for the Progressive idea of government. For the most part, the people who made up these groups were members of the maturing middle class.

Businessmen also supported this new civic philosophy. Progressivism promised a government that would help organize the economy more efficiently and provide the infrastructure critical to commerce. Business groups were interested particularly in expanding government activities that would help them. Among the most important goals of these groups was insisting that the state government take a more active role in the construction of public highways. Because of their condition, rural roads were considered an impediment to commerce, and with the introduction of automobiles at the turn of the century, the lack of a good highway system was viewed as an even greater problem. Businessmen often exercised pressure on politicians through the formation of associations, and to urge better roads they established the Arkansas Good Roads Association at Little Rock in 1903. The AGRA attracted support from prominent local businessmen, who ultimately expanded the association to include eminent politicians and businessmen from throughout the state. The association even drafted a state aid bill that was sent to the general assembly for consideration in 1903. That bill failed, but business interests continued to agitate for improved roads. This issue attracted many businessmen, but providing better schools and improving the health of Arkansans ultimately would draw even more attention from among these groups.

The growing community of professionals in Arkansas had supported more active government from the start. They had used state government to create licensing requirements for entrance into their individual fields and in some cases to regularize educational standards and curriculum necessary for practice. By the turn of the century many of these groups had begun to develop elaborate political agendas as they tried to apply their knowledge to the problems of the state. Medical people encouraged government to take a more active role to ensure the health of Arkansans. Members of the state's teacher association pushed both for increased state support of education and the development of a state system to establish mandatory educational standards. Of course the members of these professions had the expertise needed to deal with these problems.

Women played a particularly strong role in pushing for governmental reform through the women's clubs that had developed in the late nineteenth century. United in the Arkansas Federation of Women's Clubs, the local groups put forward a broad program of reform. At times the women urged legislation on issues that could be considered unique to them—including such a wide variety of matters as reforming laws that restricted women's property rights, the placement of a female physician at the State Institution for the Insane, creation of a reform school for women, and construction of restrooms in towns for rural women. Legislation that would help children, however, also received strong support from these clubs. Among the numerous programs that they advocated were the establishment of a state industrial and reform school for boys and girls, a child welfare department, child labor laws, and the use of schools as social centers. Ultimately, the scope of their interests widened and women's groups came to support the entire range of Progressive measures.

As women began to view government as the agency to produce the reforms they wanted, many advocated their participation in the election of public officials. By the 1880s some women were arguing that their participation in elections would ensure good government and promote reforms that would redound to the benefit of the state. While all women in the new clubs did not participate in the suffrage movement, most of those who advocated women's suffrage came from these organizations. The movement never really took off across the state, however, until the formation of the Political Equality League at Little Rock in 1911. The PEL was filled with middle class women led by Mary Fletcher, who was its first president, and Mrs. W. P. Hutton, its vice-president. In 1911 they managed a legislative discussion of suffrage but were not successful in securing the passage of any bills.

Women's suffrage in Arkansas matured into a significant political movement with its expansion into other areas of the state after 1914. By that year the Political Equality League had branches at Hot Springs, Pine Bluff, Augusta, Malvern, and Fayetteville. At a state convention that year, members of the league organized the Arkansas Woman Suffrage Association (AWSA), with Mrs. O. F. Ellington as president. Ellington led the fight for suffrage until 1917, and then it was carried on by Mrs. T. T. Cotnam. Women had made their right to vote a major issue of Progressive reform.

Some religious congregations also became supporters of Progressive change, seeing a more involved government as an extension of the increasing social activism that they were already exhibiting in their own churches. In Arkansas, as in the rest of the South, urban congregations particularly embraced the idea that the church had to be concerned not only with individual salvation but also had to help create a better social environment. This new reform ethic was strongest in the urban churches, where most denominations accepted what was known as the Social Gospel. Congregations undertook programs to help the poor especially, providing food, encouraging education, and even furnishing sports facilities for children; full stomachs and good job prospects helped make better Christians in their view.

In addition, churches turned to government to restrict practices that undermined the individual, the family, and the community's well being, advocating laws that would stop the consumption of alcohol, prevent gambling, ensure public morality, end political corruption, and at the same time, take care of those individuals who were unable to protect or take care of themselves.

Prohibition attracted the earliest interest of many of the groups that came to constitute the Progressive coalition. Based upon the idea that government should regulate a social activity, Prohibition was in many ways not a traditional Southern political movement, reflecting more the patterns of antebellum Northern society than anything in the South. During the 1880s, however, concern mounted that alcohol consumption was out of control. Americans had always consumed large quantities of liquor, but in the urban-industrial setting the dangers to the individual and the potential damage that could be done to family, neighbors, fellow workers, and even a business were compounded. Clearly, urban residents were the ones most concerned with drinking and pushed earliest for prohibition.

While support for prohibition was broad based, women were particularly energetic. The fight was the cause in which many women first became politically active. Club women across the state had supported local temperance organizations through the 1870s, then helped to establish the state's chapter of the Women's Christian Temperance Union (WCTU) in 1879. Temperance groups originally promoted moderate use of alcohol, but by the time the WCTU was organized its goal was prohibition. The association grew slowly but steadily through the rest of the century. By 1899 the WCTU had thirty-one local unions across the state, all located in towns. The WCTU also supported prohibition newspapers, including the *Woman's Chronicle* at Little Rock.

Despite their support of prohibition, the WCTU was not included when various men's temperance and prohibition groups united to form the Arkansas Prohibition Alliance in 1886. The refusal to include women caused some members of the Arkansas Christian Temperance Union to refrain from joining the Alliance. Despite disagreements internally over this matter, the APA was a major step toward banning the sale of alcoholic beverages in the state. Some prohibition supporters opposed turning the movement into a political one, but in 1888 the Alliance began to consider the formation of an independent political party. That goal was achieved in 1892, when the state Prohibition Party ran a candidate for governor. It continued to put forward gubernatorial candidates until 1906. Although support for prohibition was strong within the state, the Prohibition Party never attracted significant support. Arkansans remained reluctant to leave the Democratic Party, and that party's leaders made it easier for the Prohibitionists to remain Democrats as they took over the mantle of leadership in working to secure reform.

The ideas behind the Prohibition movement were tinged with morality, but the movement's rhetoric indicated clearly that they fit within the Progressive framework. The consumption of alcohol was wrong because it made men less reasonable, less rational. Government could ensure reasoned behavior among the members of society by prohibiting the manufacture and sale of alcohol. In a state prohibition meeting held at Little Rock in October 1888, the delegates asserted that "man has no moral or legal right to engage in the traffic of any article in any manner that tends to weaken or destroy the intellect given by God, and also reduces mankind below the level of the brute." The Prohibitionists hoped to "bring about a higher order of things by education" but they also believed that with an absolute ban on the sale of alcohol they would succeed in "preventing men from destroying their lives and [the] happiness of others for their own benefit."

The Progressive idea affected town governments first. During the 1880s municipal authorities had been forced to greater activity, particularly in providing essential services to the community. In every town the number of public employees grew as offices and agencies had to be created. The activities of state government had not increased as rapidly, but even there the idea of government responsibility was changing as the state helped to stabilize social relations through legislation that formally defined professions and laws that specified racial guidelines. Agrarian pressure had also pushed the general assembly to adopt a variety of laws to correct abuses by corporations, particularly railroads.

At all levels government moved toward greater regulation of community actions, but the state had not yet started to create institutions that would impose or enforce such regulations. However, a significant expansion of state power through more systematic management was taken in 1898 when the legislature created the State Railroad Commission. By that time it was clear that special regulatory legislation would never effectively control the numerous railroads within the state. These were complex corporations with intricate business operations, which no single piece of legislation could possibly deal with completely. Instead, by the mid-1890s legislators began considering the creation of a standing commission charged with overseeing the railroads.

In 1895 Joseph T. Robinson, who later as governor and United States senator continued to support Progressive legislation, introduced the first bill to create a commission. The railroads resisted it vigorously, even provoking by their actions some charges of legislative bribery. Their opposition blocked passage of Robinson's bill, but support for the idea of a commission persisted. In 1897 the general assembly again considered a commission. Rep. William F. Kirby of Texarkana, another young Progressive, became one of the bill's chief proponents. The railroads were able to defeat it again, blocking it in the state senate, but convincing Kirby that corruption had influenced the senate's action and that corporations had to be regulated. Supporters of the commission idea regrouped, pushed for a constitutional amendment to create a commission that would set railroad rates, and finally secured it with the passage of the amendment in 1898.

The new railroad commission produced only limited success at first. The original commissioners were not familiar with railroad rate setting and apparently did a bad job. Nonetheless, the commission represented a major change in the role and function of the state government. It was a permanent body exercising continuing supervision over railroad rates. In the future the commissioners, representing the public interest, would personally and with the help of a staff achieve the expertise they needed. The system promised that eventually a set of rates fair to both the railroads and the public could be established. Ultimately, the commission did bring down railroad rates within the state, and its powers over transportation continued to be expanded by subsequent legislation.

During the administration of Gov. Jeff Davis, Progressive trends continued, although no further steps were taken to change the basic operations of government in managing social problems. The general assembly passed numerous reform laws between 1901 and 1905—including restrictions on child labor in factories, a ten-hour day in lumber mills, and a reform school for youthful lawbreakers. An antitrust act passed in 1905 may have been the most important. William Kirby of Texarkana used this law to successfully prosecute companies charged with price fixing after he became attorney general in 1906. During the Davis years, however, the legislature continued the policy of special legislation designed to deal with specific problems. Progressive regulation expanded, but the idea of systematic administration of these regulations had not yet arrived.

The complete triumph of Progressivist government in Arkansas finally occurred in 1908. The election of George W. Donaghey as governor and a legislature willing to give him much of what he wanted produced a revolution in state government. Taking root in Donaghey's two terms between 1909 and 1913, the Progressive idea continued to grow during the administrations of Joseph T. Robinson and George W. Hays, then took another leap forward under Charles H. Brough (1917–1921). By the end of Brough's second term, Arkansas government had experienced a virtual revolution in its role in society. Thomas C. McRae attempted to continue the Progressive trends during his two terms from 1921 to 1925, but new conditions during the 1920s frustrated his efforts and brought a new conservatism back to Arkansas politics.

The 1908 state election indicated clearly the power of Progressivism among the electorate. Most observers considered the major candidates in the Democratic primary, George W. Donaghey and Atty. Gen. William F. Kirby, plus two minor aspirants, to be Progressives. Their platforms dealt with issues of specific concern that year, and the position of all the candidates reflected a similar attitude. All supported the establishment of agricultural schools, an end to the convict lease system used in the state penitentiary, and speedy completion of the construction of the new state capitol—a project begun in 1899, but which languished to the point of becoming a political issue. While individual candidates embraced other specific goals, there was little to distinguish among them: all promised government action.

In the campaign, Donaghey received the greatest amount of support from Progressive groups. He secured open support among the leaders of the American Federation of Labor and the Arkansas Farmers Union. His own anti-liquor position and the role that he had taken in driving saloons from Conway when he was mayor of that town gained him the support of state prohibitionists. Kirby, on the other hand, had the disadvantage of being considered too much of a politician, and his connections with Jeff Davis worked against him when Donaghey began to portray his own campaign as a fight against Davis's political machine. The election showed that Donaghey had convinced Arkansas voters that he was the most progressive candidate.

The basis for Donaghey's triumph, even though he secured support throughout the state, was his strength in the towns and cities. He and the other Progressives were personally rooted in the communities' middle class. Rather than a lawyer, as successful gubernatorial candidates typically were, Donaghey came from a business background. A carpenter with training as an architect and structural engineer, he had made a small fortune constructing public buildings throughout the Southwest and as one of the principal contractors of the Choctaw, Oklahoma, and Gulf Railroad. While Governors Robinson and Hays represented a return to traditional politicians, Charles Brough was a teacher with a Ph.D. from Johns Hopkins University. Thomas McRae had been an attorney, a state legislator, and a member of Congress, but when elected he was a banker. Progressivism brought a new type of leader to the fore.

These governors repeatedly affirmed their commitment to Progressive ideas about government and its operations. To them, government had to be reorganized and made more efficient. The example these politicians used as their model was business: "Having seen what efficiency can accomplish in industrial and business affairs," Donaghey told members of the Thirty-Seventh Legislature in his inaugural address, "I am now prepared to believe that even so important a work as statecraft is only an intensely practical matter." Later, in his first inaugural, Charles Brough pledged to have an "administration based on efficiency, political ideals characterized by purity and a democracy ennobled by achievement."

Between 1908 and 1925 a flood of legislation tried to produce a government that was practical and efficient and solved the profusion of problems facing the state and its people. As a result, politics itself changed. People accepted a wider definition of the proper services the state should provide. Regulatory functions expanded. Ultimately, state government began to play a greater role in the study of economic and social problems and in proposing and advocating solutions. As the Progressives hypothesized, government could direct the course of a community's development.

Changes in the state's political life were one of the legacies of the Progressives. The creation of a Democratic primary was considered a major step toward ending corruption in elections. That law was amended and strengthened repeatedly.

The state also moved to extend greater powers of self-government to towns and cities. A 1913 law established the commission form of government for first-class cities. That same year, town people were given the right of referendum on ordinances passed by city governments.

Women and their supporters finally secured the franchise. Against strong opposition, the AWSA successfully lobbied legislation through the general assembly. In 1915 they finally managed to get the legislature to submit a constitutional amendment to popular vote in the 1916 general election. It was not, however, on the ballot. The next year the legislature moved to allow women the vote in primary elections; Arkansas women first cast their ballots in the May 1918 Democratic primary. Full victory did not come until the women's suffrage amendment to the United States Constitution and a similar amendment to the state constitution were adopted in 1920.

Another major political accomplishment was a constitutional amendment allowing the initiative and referendum. The campaign for that measure showed to a certain degree both the coalition that was behind Progressivism by this time and the forces that opposed it. Proponents of the amendment argued that it provided for more direct democracy and allowed the people to act on their own against the "interests" that too often controlled the general assembly. The measure attracted support not only from Donaghey but also from the state chapter of the American Federation of Labor and the Arkansas Farmers Union.

The opponents of the initiative and referendum ideologically attacked the measure as an effort at overthrowing the system of checks and balances that had been built into the national and state constitutional systems. They were right, and in fact the system of checks and balances had traditionally been used to protect some minorities from what many conservatives considered to be the tyranny of the majority. It was not surprising, then, when in the election the state's major urban areas and most of the upland areas supported the amendment, while the cotton-belt counties filled with blacks opposed the measure.

In the end, the one reform many Progressives considered essential, the writing of a new constitution, was defeated. Pushed by Progressive leaders such as Governor Brough, the legislature provided for a constitutional convention in the fall of 1917. As written, it included many of the ideas embraced by the Progressives, among them being women's suffrage, prohibition, and major changes in the tax system. Charges that the proposed constitution would raise taxes were central to its defeat, leaving Progressive reform as a patch of special legislation rather than the system they would have desired.

While Progressives devoted a considerable effort to reforming government itself, the bulk of their legislation was designed to improve the lot of Arkansas through the regulation of a variety of behaviors and practices considered to be abusive or destructive of the lives of Arkansans. Prohibition, long a reform issue, finally secured enough support for legislation to be enacted. In 1916 Prohibition forces got a bill through the legislature that ended the sale of licenses for selling liquor and also prohibited the manufacturing and sale of liquor. The next year, the legislature passed the "Bone Dry" law, prohibiting the shipment of alcoholic beverages into the state.

The general assembly also established a massive body of legislation regulating the economy, particularly limiting the power of large corporations. The Anti-Trust Act of 1905 was revised and amended. A 1915 "Blue Sky" law established regulations for the sale of stocks and bonds to prevent fraud. These measures also included statutes to regulate labor conditions. In 1909 a law was passed requiring corporations to pay employees at least twice a month. An employer liability act was passed. In 1917 the legislature established a free employment bureau under the commissioner of labor.

Other laws attempted to protect individuals in society who were unable to protect themselves—particularly children and women. Children were the main beneficiary of such measures. In 1911 a juvenile court system was created to take children out of the regular courts. An initiated act ratified in the 1914 general election forbade the employment of minors in certain occupations. In 1915 the legislature established a minimum wage for women and enacted regulations over their working hours. That same legislature removed the disabilities of married women. Up to this point a married woman surrendered her rights to have property or make contracts. The new laws ensured that a married woman continued to have such economic rights.

It is worth noting that the one problem area that received almost no attention was the issue of race. Progressivism was essentially racist. This does not mean that they were unwilling to protect African-Americans to some degree from the worst abuses. In 1909, for example, the general assembly passed a law designed to end the practice of nightriding, usually a violent attack upon blacks. While accepting the idea that African-Americans might be better educated and have their lives improved, however, white Progressives refused to accept the idea that they were equals and should be treated so.

Government was made purer, legislation offered greater protection to people, and the services provided by the state were increased. A more lasting impact of Progressivism, however, may have been the expansion of old and the creation of new state agencies to implement all of the new regulations and placing these government departments into the hands of professional staffs. Their idea was to take many governmental operations out of politics so that career professionals could develop reasoned and efficient solutions to the state's problems.

The state penitentiary was one of the traditional agencies that was radically changed. Prison reform had been a major concern for decades, and the practice of leasing convicts to private companies was considered one of the most iniquitous problems in the way that the prisons were managed.

Developed in the 1870s to make the prisons pay for themselves, the system had been subjected to considerable abuse by companies that employed workers, especially the western mines. In addition, free laborers objected to the use of convicts in any business where they competed directly.

In 1911 Governor Donaghey proposed an end to the system during a special session of the general assembly. He wanted one-third of the convicts put to work on a state farm, where they would raise food and farm products for their own support, and the rest put to work on the state's roads. Donaghey's ideas reflected those of professional penologists who had come to understand prisons as institutions of reform rather than punishment alone. Donaghey's first efforts proved fruitless. While many convicts were committed to the state farm, the old Cummins plantation in Lincoln County, the legislature refused to abolish the policy of hiring out surplus convicts not engaged in farming. Only after a dramatic pardoning of 360 convicts in 1912 and a full-scale attack upon the lease system by the governor was anything accomplished, and Donaghey's successor was able to secure an end to the leasing system through the legislature in February 1913.

Old agencies were reformed, and a wide variety of new ones were created. Other than constitutional officers, the state had possessed little governmental apparatus as late as the turn of the century. By the end of the Progressive era, however, much of the actual work of the state was carried out by a variety of new commissions and departments. As a result of Progressive legislation, by 1920 Arkansas had a tax commission; a state health department; a state high school board; a state bank department; a highway commission; a bureau of labor statistics; a commission to regulate assessments on railroads, express, sleeping car, telegraph, and telephone companies; a department of insurance and fire protection; the Arkansas Corporation Commission; and the Commission of Charities and Corrections. As with the Railroad Commission, the legislature gave these institutions a major role in the direction of state affairs.

Three areas received much of the attention of governors and legislators—education, health, and transportation. A more in-depth look at how government changed in dealing with problems in these areas shows how the new system operated. It also indicates the results produced by the bureaucratic approach.

Improving Arkansas's schools may have been one of the most important problems faced at the turn of the century. Agricultural conditions indicated clearly that there was not a bright future for people who remained on the farm. Opportunities existed in the cities of Arkansas and outside the state, but education was essential to take advantage of these. Although the state encouraged schools and had a superintendent of education, there was actually no overall system. Instead, every local school district financed and controlled its own schools. As a result, educational conditions across the state varied greatly, and serious inequities existed between urban and rural schools, white and black schools, and rich and poor districts.

Through the late nineteenth century, state school superintendents were usually content simply to report the condition of state schools. By the turn of the century, however, these reports were increasingly critical. In 1902 the state superintendent of public instruction criticized the fragmentation of the existing system, asking for at least the unification of county schools under a single county supervisor. His explanations for the recommendation showed that Progressive ideas about schools had made an impact on educators. "It is conceded," reported J. J. Doyne, "that no business enterprise can prosper without there shall be some one at its head, charged with its general conduct and control." Doyne observed that teachers might do their best, but "with no one at the head of the system, whose business it shall be to unify the work, to outline methods of procedure, to arrange course of study, to aid by timely suggestions to the teachers, to keep them acquainted with the general progress of the work in the county, to look after the making out of such reports as shall give an intelligent conception of the status of educational affairs, the highest results cannot be secured from their labor." The schools lacked order necessary for efficiency and that had to be changed.

The theme of centralization and concentration in order to improve the education of Arkansas's children recurred throughout the Progressive years. The state teacher's association accepted the idea that problems could be resolved through reason and became a major force pushing for studies by the state and private commissions to analyze and offer solutions for school problems. In 1908, the association was instrumental in securing support from the Southern Education Board for the creation of the Arkansas Educational Commission to report on the condition of schools in the state. It was also crucial in the establishment of the Arkansas Illiteracy Commission in 1917.

These organizations produced proposals that the teacher's association, state superintendents, and ultimately special boards attempted to implement. The report of the Arkansas Educational Commission, issued in 1911, laid out a comprehensive plan of reforms to strengthen public education.

Citing the need for compulsory school attendance, consolidation of the large number of school districts, and greater financial aid for high schools, the commission also urged the establishment of a state board of education to continue systematic planning and control over the public schools. In its findings, the Arkansas Illiteracy Commission, created by the legislature in 1917 to recommend a plan to reduce illiteracy, also asserted the need for central direction in school operations.

Although a true system never developed, between 1900 and 1920 the schools experienced significant change. The legislature allowed districts to borrow money to improve their facilities. Compulsory attendance was mandated. In 1909 the legislature established a system of agricultural schools in the state. In almost every session, the legislature enacted some measures dealing with education. The closest thing to the creation of a centralized system came with the creation of the state high school board in 1911, when it was authorized to perform duties of administration until the creation of a state board of education. The high school board was given enormous power over the classification of high schools, determination of curriculum, and distribution of aid dedicated to the improvement of normal departments— departments designed to train teachers. The legislature resisted efforts to eliminate local school districts or to deprive them of their autonomy, however. Local interests were reluctant to surrender control over taxation in all cases, and school taxes could be potentially large.

Nonetheless, efforts at improving the state's schools were remarkably successful. Between 1900 and 1920 the percentage of children of scholastic age who were actually in class increased from 64 percent to 71 percent. The average school term increased from 77 days to 126 days, and the amount of money spent on education rose from $3.64 per pupil to $15.73. Even teacher salaries improved, with the wage of a Grade I male instructor increasing from $38 to $90 per month.

Statistics on illiteracy, the one measurement that clearly showed the impact of education, indicated that these changes were having positive consequences for the people of Arkansas. At the turn of the century, 20.4 percent of Arkansans ten years of age or older were illiterate. By 1909 the state reported 13.5 percent of that population illiterate. In 1919 this number had dropped to 9.4 percent statewide. Even though educators had not been able to put in place all of the reforms that they sought, those they had succeeded in having adopted produced obvious positive results.

By the 1920s it was no longer possible to point to education as a problem in general, but there were still areas where improvement was needed. A 1923 report by the national Bureau of Education concluded that rural schools still lagged behind the schools in the towns. An even greater problem was the fact that education for African-Americans lagged far behind that of whites. While overall school enrollment had improved between 1900 and 1920, black enrollments remained at about 62 percent of scholastic-aged children. The money spent on black schools and teacher's salaries was only about two-thirds of that spent for whites.

The failure to bring more blacks into the educational system and to give black schools the resources to keep up with white standards had a clear social cost. The 1900 census reported 43 percent of African-Americans ten years old or above as illiterate. That rate was cut drastically by 1909 to 26.4 percent, although this was still nearly three times that for the general population. In the 1910s, however, progress virtually ceased. By 1919 the portion of illiterate African-Americans was still 21.8 percent.

The state also adopted a Progressive approach on health issues, although never giving state health officials complete control over local health matters. In 1913 the legislature had created a state board of health, consisting of an appointed board supported by a professional staff. Before 1920 the board's tasks had been greatly expanded—it carried out health initiatives backed by private agencies or the federal government; collected vital statistics; supervised health inspections of hotels, restaurants, and water and sewer systems; and developed plans for the overall improvement of the health of Arkansans.

As in the case of the schools, the state health agency made an enormous impact on the lives of Arkansans. Although not the problem in Arkansas that it was in many other Southern states, hookworm was virtually eradicated in the state with funding from the Rockefeller Foundation. Inspections of water supplies and sanitary conditions practically eliminated typhoid fever. In cooperation with the state teacher's association and the Arkansas Federation of Women's Clubs, a program to improve home and school sanitation was pursued. Another Rockefeller Foundation–funded program sought to eliminate malaria through mosquito control. In 1919 the board began a vigorous educational campaign against venereal disease after thousands of infected Arkansans were unable to join the army. By the 1920s the board had turned to an effective program for improving the health of infants and mothers with funding from the federal government under the Sheppard-Towner Act. Throughout Arkansas, the infant death rate declined and life expectancy increased.

The third major initiative undertaken by the state was the development of good highways, a task that was placed in the hands of the State Highway Commission and a highway department. Again, the commission consisted of an appointed board backed by a professional staff. The highway department would establish "uniform plans and specifications" for projects throughout the state and ultimately provide guidelines within which a highway system could be developed. Almost immediately the department pushed for changes in funding, allowing county highway taxes to be expended anywhere in the county rather than only in the district where they were collected. "System in road matters is as necessary as in any private business, yet we are in the same rut and have been for forty years," was the conclusion of the first highway engineer.

Although the new department was never able to create a true state system, highways across Arkansas did improve under its supervision. By 1920 the government finally managed to secure statewide funding for a major road development through the creation of the Arkansas-Louisiana Highway Improvement District, and with those funds built the first hard-surfaced road through the state, 156 miles long, 18 feet wide, costing $3,100,000.

Progressives expanded state activities, though at a cost. The biennial budget for the state in 1899–1900 had been approximately $2.5 million. The budget by 1919–1920 had risen to $15.5 million. The amount spent on every department increased. Expenditures in the governor's office rose from $14,000 to $34,000. Ultimately, however, the increase in the state budget was due to the formation of the numerous new agencies, boards, commissions, and departments. It was clear by 1920 that Progressive Arkansas cost money and that the central problem facing Arkansas's politicians then was the same as it had been in 1874: how to pay for government in a community where propertied interests resisted any increases in taxes. Governor after governor pointed out raising sufficient revenue to run the government as a significant challenge. Governor Hays, in his 1915 address to the general assembly, singled out revenue collection as the "most serious problem" that confronted the state.

A major part of this revenue crisis was not tax rates but tax assessments, which all experts considered to be inequitable. Under the Constitution of 1874, control over both assessments and appeals of assessments were left to the county courts, a body that would only reluctantly override the claims of prominent local citizens, and many wealthy landowners either underassessed the value of their land or did not report it at all. In 1911 Governor Donaghey pushed for the adoption of the Turner-Jacobsen Revenue Bill in the general assembly. It called for statewide reassessments and placed appeals under the authority of a state tax commission and the circuit courts. The bill passed, but it had to be voted on in the 1912 election.

That year Donaghey ran for a third term as governor, at least in part to campaign for the passage of the Turner-Jacobsen Bill. Donaghey's bid for a third term showed the danger any effort at changing tax policies within the state posed for a candidate. In the campaign, the reevaluation of property provided a major point upon which Donaghey was attacked by his political enemies and probably led to his defeat. Joseph T. Robinson, a four-term congressman from Lonoke, ran against Donaghey, charging that the Turner-Jacobsen Bill increased taxes and placed too much power in the hands of central authority. Robinson proclaimed himself an advocate of low taxes and insisted that he would work to cut the cost of state government and limit its spending to only its income. Although Robinson was practically indistinguishable from Donaghey as a Progressive—his campaign emphasized limiting campaign expenditures, restricting lobbyists, reforming the prisons, and expanding the use of the initiative, the referendum, and the recall—he was able to use fiscal conservatism to defeat the governor.

The struggle to secure adequate financing for state programs continued under Gov. George Hays. In 1915 Hays emphasized again the inequities of the assessment system, pointing to the fact that the federal census evaluated property in the state at $1.5 billion, while the tax rolls showed an assessed evaluation of only $450 million. Even though Hays asked for reassessment, Robinson's campaign in 1912 had made all politicians reluctant to touch the problem. No one did. In 1917 Gov. Charles H. Brough also asked the legislature to consider the problem of revenue, telling its members that "a thoroughgoing revision of [the] revenue system is the paramount question confronting our lawmakers." Brough made headway in stabilizing the finances of the state, but the legislature continued its traditional resistance to any changes in the assessment process or increases in taxes. Much of what was accomplished came through restricting program expenses and raising revenues with special taxes and fees charged for a variety of state services. Brough, like his predecessors, was unable to bring about any serious restructuring of the state tax system.

Ultimately, Arkansas government experienced a revolution in the way it operated after the beginning of the twentieth century. In fact, the new form of government with its emphasis upon professional agencies and systematic planning in addressing state problems was producing significant results. In particular, educational and health initiatives were improving the lives of many Arkansans. Education was singularly important, offering the prospect that many rural Arkansans might escape the limits and problems of the agricultural economy. Such changes had only begun, however, when renewed economic problems following the end of World War I undermined the entire effort. In the end, not only government efforts at improving Arkansas but the entire economy of growth and change that seemed to have made Arkansas a part of the New South crumbled in the midst of the crises of the 1920s.

The End of an Era

The end of World War I saw a major reversal in the fortunes of Arkansans. While in some economic areas growth continued, even this progress, integrating the state and its people into larger national trends, produced destabilization and contributed to fear. The very forces that had brought about economic development in the years following the farmers' revolt now brought about a major crisis for many of the state's citizens. Agriculture, which had only recently emerged from the depression of the 1880s and 1890s, was hard hit. This time, however, the townspeople who had seemed immune from the earlier crises were also involved. The 1920s would be marked by a continuing economic confrontation with problems of the evolving national market, a confrontation that contributed to a major social crisis as well.

The war's end produced serious difficulties for the state's economy in general. Prices for many of the state's products declined, and in some cases demand virtually disappeared. The immediate results were hard times for farmers and layoffs in industry. Disputes between labor and management were almost inevitable in such a situation. Economic troubles did little to encourage optimistic views of the future and contributed to uncertainty and fear throughout the community.

Of all the potential problems, the collapse of prewar and wartime prices for agricultural commodities was the most readily apparent at the war's end, affecting the largest number of people in Arkansas. There were numerous factors involved in what took place. Grain prices fell as a result of the end of World War I as European nations restored their own food production capabilities, thus eliminating one of the markets that had driven them up after 1914. Prices also declined because increasing productivity on midwestern wheat and corn farms had caused supplies to outpace the growth of demand. Even though Arkansas farms had not matched the increasing productivity of farms elsewhere, local farmers sold their crops in the same market and received the same low prices. Between 1919 and 1921 corn prices fell one dollar to fifty-two cents per bushel, then recovered and remained in the vicinity of eighty cents for the rest of the decade. Wheat prices dropped over the same period from $2.13 per bushel to $1.00, afterward fluctuating up to $1.40.

The state's orchard farmers were hit perhaps harder than anyone. After decades of work building up a significant operation, during the 1920s the state's orchards were nearly wiped out. As in the case of other crops, integration into the national market showed that it could have a dark side when increasing fruit production in the northwest drove prices down to the point that Arkansas growers were no longer competitive. Poor weather and pests added to the problem. In 1929 apple orchards, which harvested over 7 million bushels in 1919, gathered only about 1.5 million bushels. Other crops had equally bad years.

Rice, another commodity that had offered some farmers the promise of better times, also experienced a sharp drop in prices. Those who had fully converted to rice culture found themselves in much the same shape as other farmers in the state. With fewer persons raising rice and with cultivation taking place in a relatively smaller area of the state, rice growers were able to create cooperatives through which to market their crops. The boom was over, but through cooperative action rice farmers were able to remain in relatively better shape than many others.

The situation for cotton looked even more disastrous at the beginning of the 1920s. Long-term consumer tastes were changing and driving down demand. Rayon, a synthetic fiber, had been introduced into the United States in 1911, but its physical characteristics had delayed its general acceptance in clothing. By 1920, however, finer and stronger filaments could be used to manufacture cloth that appeared to be much more durable than cotton and was more acceptable in clothing. Synthetic materials gained an increasing share of the market. As the demand for cotton went down, so did the price. In 1920 market specialists predicted that the year's crop would sell for forty cents per pound. Instead, by the end of September the price of cotton had dropped to six cents per pound.

Cotton farmers were also faced with natural impediments through the 1920s. Weather was a continuing problem, with several bad springs during the decade. Then in the spring of 1927 a major flood along the Mississippi River washed out roads and bridges and forced thousands to rely on state and federal assistance. In addition, by 1924 a variety of insect pests had spread throughout the cotton lands of the state. The boll weevil entered the new lands opened in the earlier part of the century. Red spiders also appeared. Farmers on small holdings simply did not have the resources to fight these destructive creatures; insecticides were still only in limited use, and the poorer farmer could not afford anything at all.

Given the prices of other commodities and despite the weakness of the cotton market, the 1920s saw more and more farmers turn to cotton as their principal cash crop. In the mid-1920s prices steadied and then rose again. Although they remained far below the wartime highs, prices ranged between 28.69 cents per pound in 1923 to a low of 12.49 cents in 1926. While attempting to stabilize their financial situation, farmers fastened cotton production on the state even more firmly as they devoted nearly 3.5 million acres to its cultivation in 1929 compared to 2.8 million acres in 1919.

Clearly, farmers were in trouble. Still, hard times had happened before and most continued their struggle with the land, hoping that prices might turn around and the prosperity of earlier decades would return. For those who remained on the farms, there was little to do but keep on working. Some innovation took place. Farmers continued to seek new marketable crops that would allow them to move away from the economically stagnant traditional ones. Some began to make more use of tractors (replacing mule-drawn plows), which allowed them to cut deeper furrows and, at least for a time, increase productivity. Others expanded their use of fertilizers. Most of these innovations cost money, however, and few had the financial resources to be very experimental.

Occasional successes hardly overcame the overwhelming drift of the agricultural economy toward a depression. Economic circumstances were clearly evidenced in the collapse of farm values during the 1920s. After having more than doubled in value between 1910 and 1920 and reaching over $753 million in total worth, the bottom dropped out. By 1930 the collective value of the state's farms had fallen to approximately $547 million, a loss of over 27 percent.

Other conditions indicated that although the collapse of prices was central to the problems of the 1920s, the situation actually represented a continuation of trends that had never abated even in the good times. Farm size continued to disintegrate into less-efficient units, dropping between 1920 and 1930 from an average of 75 acres to 66. Tenancy continued to rise, moving from 51 percent in 1920 to 63 percent by 1930. Farm mortgages also grew, with nearly 38 percent of holdings securing loans by the end of the decade.

During the 1920s the new industries that had developed over the previous forty-five years joined agriculture in an economic decline. The reasons were complex and each industry had different factors at work. In the timber industry, many companies found that by the 1920s they had practically exhausted the lands at hand. Most of them simply ceased operations and moved elsewhere. In 1919 there had been 1,506 companies in the state; by 1929 that number had dropped to 625. Nearly ten thousand people lost their jobs as a result.

Larger lumber companies began to experiment with ways to keep their lands in production, shifting from simply cutting virgin forests to actually raising timber as well. In 1926 the Crossett Company hired its first professional forester from the program at Yale University and began the practice of harvesting trees according to their growth rate, thus establishing a continuing supply. This plus other forms of scientific management ensured that the lumber industry would remain a vital part of the state's economy into future decades and increased the possibilities of long-term profits. It also meant that larger companies survived while smaller operations were either bought out or failed.

The state's bauxite mines also were seriously affected by a drastic fall in prices immediately following the end of the war. Peace allowed French bauxite production to resume. Military demand for aluminum products dropped sharply and civilian consumption did not move in to maintain demand. In 1920 and 1921 the mines reduced production and laid off large numbers of laborers. By 1922 aluminum companies employed only about four hundred workers in central Arkansas. Price stabilization after 1921 meant that the mines continued to operate, but at a rate of production much reduced from the previous decade.

The coal industry faced hard times as demand decreased after the war, in part because of the emergence of petroleum as a fuel. The number of companies and workers engaged in coal mining did not decrease, but there was increasing pressure to cut wages. In October 1919, when mine owners nationally attempted to force wages down, Arkansas miners joined the nationwide strike by the United Mine Workers. In December the strike ended with a 27 percent increase in wages. The victory was only short-lived, however. Declining demand for coal gave management increasing leverage in its dealings with labor, so that by 1927 the mines that had been controlled by UMW were all operating on an open shop system, and wages had been cut to 1917 standards.

Even the Arkansas oil boom that occurred in the early 1920s had a short life, but produced an economic bonanza for some residents. One estimate places the amount of money invested in the development of the Arkansas fields and facilities during their first five years of operation at some $600 million. Bringing seventy cents per barrel in 1921, there was money to be made. Ultimately, however, the prosperity was fleeting. The initial discoveries were of shallow oil pockets, and given the practice of letting wells run at their full capacity, the original fields were depleted within roughly five years. Oil continued to be a major part of the state's industrial product, but its importance remained regional; it never became the same liberating economic force it was in neighboring Louisiana and Texas.

Manufacturing also suffered serious setbacks in the 1920s. Between 1919 and 1921 the state lost nearly 60 percent of its manufacturing companies in almost every area of industrial effort. This cost some sixteen thousand jobs, nearly one-third of all manufacturing employment.

A major part of manufacturing's problem was that many of the operations were connected somehow to the agricultural economy. Most shops and factories either processed farm products or provided goods to the farm-dominated local economy. Processing industries whose charges were related to the price of farm commodities were directly affected by the collapse of agricultural prices. In the case of fruit processing, companies literally had nothing to process and were forced out of business. For those manufacturing goods aimed at the rural economy, the market contracted substantially. Even the Climber Automobile Company, producing its cars for Southerners, was unable to survive in a regional market where 80 percent of its potential customers were farmers in the middle of serious economic difficulties.

This general economic decline did not mean that there was a complete end to progress. By the mid-1920s some prices stabilized. Farming and most of the extractive industries remained in trouble, but manufacturing slowly recovered. Even though hit hard, manufacturing proved much more resilient than the state's other industries through the decade.

This was in part due to the development of electrical utilities, which promoted industrial growth in order to increase demand for its own product. While electricity had been introduced into cities in the closing years of the nineteenth century, the countryside had remained without power. During the 1920s changes in the national industry, particularly the introduction of bigger power plants, made systems that served larger markets more efficient and potentially profitable. Therefore, in 1926 and in combination with rival Arkansas power officials, National Power and Light, which operated Little Rock's electrical system, consolidated a number of smaller systems across the state into Arkansas Power and Light Company, headed by Harvey C. Couch. AP&L began constructing dams to generate hydroelectric power and introduced electricity throughout the state. This allowed manufacturing companies to locate virtually anywhere in Arkansas.

By the end of the decade, much of the earlier losses in manufacturing had been regained; by 1929 all but three thousand of the jobs lost after 1919 were replaced. The actual value of the state's manufactured products increased during the 1920s, rising from approximately $200 million to $211 million. In his inaugural address in January 1927, Gov. John E. Martineau could actually say: "Our State is believed by many to be upon the eve of a long deferred industrial awakening." That awakening was not realized because of events after 1929, but manufacturing seemed to have survived its first real economic downturn.

The economic reversal had far-reaching social implications for Arkansans, too. Across the state thousands who had been employed in the expanding industries were now without jobs. Farmers found themselves reduced once again to poverty. Responses varied, but the most readily apparent was the movement of many Arkansans either to towns or, in even larger numbers, out of state. During the 1920s, growth of the farm population came to a standstill. Towns experienced some increase, although not at the same rate as in previous decades, but many Arkansans seemed to be moving on. In some ways, Progressive education might be considered a real success. Aware of greater opportunities elsewhere and now armed with at least a few skills that allowed them to compete in urban-industrial markets, young Arkansans headed for the far west to seek new opportunities. In the long run, this was probably good—the move away from the farm, essential for agricultural stabilization, had begun.

For those who stayed, the future must have seemed much less certain. Fears generated by economic problems were compounded by other challenges that seemed to overwhelm communities. In areas affected by the oil industry, society was in turmoil. Beggars drifted to the towns seeking handouts, and entrepreneurs offering oil workers twenty-five-cent dancing, gambling, prostitution, and alcoholic beverages proliferated in the area.

For businessmen, other problems rivaled immorality as a social evil. Labor unions such as the IWW appeared in southern Arkansas, trying to organize oil-field workers. Unions also continued to thrive in the mining country and among farm workers. While success was always limited, this continuing effort was seen by those who desired stability in the labor force as a serious threat.

Perhaps even more disconcerting for white Arkansans than immorality or union activity was an increasing assertiveness by African-Americans. The wartime experiences of some and the appearance in the state of organizations, such as the National Association for the Advancement of Colored People, that encouraged African-Americans to resist unfair labor practices and stand up against discrimination probably contributed to this new attitude. For whatever reason, blacks showed increasing resistance when dealing with what they felt was unfair treatment. At Dumas in January 1920, when authorities tried to arrest a man charged with killing a hog on a plantation, local blacks protected him. Ultimately, federal troops were sent to the county to help the local sheriff make arrests.

The general sense of social crisis was increased by the ways whites reacted to what they perceived as aggressiveness by blacks. When a young black man, charged with the murder of a white landowner whom he believed had cheated him, was found in Texas and brought back to Arkansas, he was kidnapped from the train, returned to Nodena in Mississippi County, and burned alive. The county sheriff was conveniently absent in Memphis at the time. No one in that mob was ever prosecuted. Whites had made the point clear that blacks would be treated outside the law if they stepped beyond accepted racial bounds.

All of the things taking place at home were made even more frightening by the Russian Revolution, the Bolshevik triumph in 1918, and the development of what many Americans feared was a conspiracy to overthrow democracy and capitalism. It was easy to see prostitutes, the IWW, and the NAACP as part of some devious plot to destroy their whole way of life.

Increasing fears caused many Arkansas to view a breakdown of law and order as the state's greatest problem by 1921. That January, Gov. Thomas C. McRae proclaimed "Law and Order Sunday" to promote observance of the law. Change had destroyed an orderly society and had provided the framework within which lawbreakers and criminals thrived. Clearly, somehow, the system was not controlling the population. It was being taken advantage of by everyone from "wily lawyers" to "sob sister jurors." Many concluded that severe and certain punishment had to be imposed on criminals to force a new respect for the law. In fact, this threat, perceived by so many Arkansans, reflected no real increase in criminal behavior. Instead, it mirrored their own need to bring about some order in a world that had suddenly gone awry.

It is not surprising that many Arkansans began to look to religion for an explanation of what was taking place and for a solution to the crisis. The conclusion for many was that what they called religious "liberalism" or "modernism," which denied an absolute truth and argued for tolerance of views, was at the heart of the problem. It forced the community to tolerate behaviors never accepted in the rural neighborhoods of the past, raised questions, and challenged the status quo, undermining any clear sense of order.

The growing backlash against "modernity" in Arkansas was reflected primarily in the rise of religious fundamentalism during the 1920s, a doctrine that attacked the central tenant of modernist ideology: that change was possible, that the world and ideas were not immutable, and that this change was not only inevitable but desirable and could even be directed by society. Emerging in the late nineteenth century, fundamentalism took the offensive against modernism in 1909, when a group calling themselves Conservative Protestants united and began publishing a series of pamphlets on the "fundamentals." The fundamentalists argued that their religion was based on five basic principles: the inerrancy of the Bible, the virgin birth, the atonement, the resurrection, and the second coming of Christ. In 1916 supporters of this idea formed the World's Christian Fundamentals Association at Montrose, Pennsylvania, in order to assert these elementary premises in religion and to check what it considered to be anti-Christian tendencies in many churches.

The course of fundamentalism within individual Arkansas churches is impossible to follow, but through the 1920s it clearly became more important. Its developing power was readily apparent in the attack staged upon teaching the theory of evolution in public schools in 1924. Probably few of those who became active in the anti-evolution movement knew much about the scientific theory they opposed. What they did know, however, was that the idea threatened the viewpoint that an infallible Bible, literally interpreted, provided clear and immutable guidelines to life. If evolution was true, then the Biblical story of creation was not literally true, therefore none of the Bible might be true. Truth and all other aspects of society, consequently, might be relative. As they could see in their day-to-day lives, such an idea only bred chaos and the destruction of social order.

While anti-evolutionist sentiment was expressed earlier, the first major step toward making the theory's teaching a public issue came in 1924 when the Arkansas State Baptist Convention rejected the theory of evolution. By 1926 legislators began to receive petitions requesting an anti-evolution law similar to one that had already been passed in Tennessee. In January 1927, supported by Rev. Ben M. Bogard, pastor of the Antioch Missionary Baptist Church in Little Rock and chairman of his congregation's anti-evolution committee, and Rev. James Seth Compere, editor of the Arkansas Baptist State Convention's *Baptist Advocate,* Rep. Astor L. Rotenberry of Pulaski County began the debate in Arkansas when he introduced a bill in the general assembly that prohibited the theory of evolution from being taught in public schools.

The Rotenberry Bill became the object of a major fight in the state legislature. Representatives of the American Association of University Professors at the University of Arkansas led the fight against the bill, arguing that it unconstitutionally prevented freedom of thought and imposed a religious test upon teachers. They were supported by student organizations at Fayetteville, who feared being shunned by graduate and medical schools where they might desire further education if the law passed. Additional support came from leaders of churches that had embraced the modernist theology. They were opposed in the legislative fight by representatives of major churches throughout the state. By the very individuals who gathered on either side, the disparate forces at work in Arkansas were made clear.

Rotenberry's bill did not pass the legislature, but its supporters decided to submit it to the public in an initiated act. Rev. Ben Bogard took the lead in agitating for the bill, incorporating the American Anti-Evolution Association, and creating a statewide organization. He promised that evolution would be an issue in every race, from governor to constable and urged all who believed in the Bible to go to the polls and ensure an end to evolutionary teaching. In the November 1928 general election, an anti-evolution law was passed as an initiated act and carried the state, 108,991 voting for to 63,406 against. The act lost in only five counties, one being highly urbanized Pulaski County. The vote on evolution, perhaps more than any other single political act, showed the rise of the new fundamentalist view across the state.

Ultimately, the increasingly conservative tenor of social debate within the community produced conservative politics. The continued reluctance to accept any change that would threaten the basic underpinning of society also manifested itself in the emergence of the Ku Klux Klan in the state in the 1920s. The Klan of the 1920s originated in Atlanta, Georgia, in 1915. Originally created by William J. Simmons, who sought to develop a new fraternity based on his own romantic view of the Ku Klux Klan of the era of Reconstruction, it had evolved into an organization dedicated to upholding traditional moral values and attacking all they considered to be un-American. Among the latter were Catholics, Jews, Negroes, foreigners, radicals, bootleggers, prostitutes, adulterers, wife beaters, crooked politicians, and a host of others. Capitalizing on postwar disillusionment and fears, the new Klan suddenly took off, with membership rapidly increasing and local Klans spreading across the nation.

KKK efforts at creating an organization in Arkansas began at Little Rock in the summer of 1921, but development was slower than in many other Southern states. By December, Klans at Gurdon, Hot Springs, Malvern, Prescott, Russellville, and Little Rock indicated their existence when they made donations to local Christmas funds. Charles C. Alexander, the most important historian of the organization in Arkansas, found that within the state it expressed many of the same feelings of hostility toward Catholics, Jews, radical labor organizers, and blacks as emphasized elsewhere. These, however, were not the driving force behind Klan success. Instead, the Arkansas Klan appears primarily to have been concerned with the challenge to nineteenth-century social order posed by the rise of the city, the advent of bootlegging, and a general deterioration in morals that followed the war. Hundreds of Arkansans expressed their fears by joining the Klan.

By early 1922 the KKK was making newspaper headlines with threats, intimidations, and floggings aimed at driving bootleggers, gamblers, fornicators, and other undesirables out of local communities. In Texarkana a young black man was forced into an automobile, driven out of town and whipped for allegedly "fooling around" with a white woman. A young white man at Nashville was killed while resisting Klan members intent on whip-

ping him for associating with black women. A Little Rock pool hall opera-
tor, a Hope bootlegger, and a Clarksville garageman all received visits from
Klansmen, who accused them of wrongdoing and beat them. In November
1922 some two hundred Klansmen in Union County attacked and burned
gambling halls, saloons, and brothels around Smackover. The Ouachita
County sheriff estimated the vigilantes had driven some 2,000 "undesirables" out of the oil fields.

According to KKK leaders, hundreds of Arkansans rushed to join them in
their attacks upon immorality. The Little Rock Klan had its first public initi-
ation ceremony near Sweet Home in February 1922, attracting more than a
thousand members and prospective initiates. By the summer of 1922 the
Grand Dragon of the state KKK claimed that there were 104 Klans in the
state and that 25,000 men had joined the organization. Klan No. 1, the
Little Rock unit, claimed to have a membership at this time of some 4,500
members. With such numbers, the leadership quickly concluded that it had
greater potential for enforcing its sense of morality on the community than
through the use of random violence, and they turned increasingly toward
politics as an avenue for their agenda.

This shift to political action by the KKK had been encouraged at the
national level by Hiram W. Evans, a Texas Klan leader who gained control
over the national organization as Imperial Wizard in 1922. In Arkansas, the
Little Rock Klan achieved its first political triumph in the city elections that
April, when their write-in candidate for alderman defeated a Catholic who
was the regular Democratic nominee. In the August Democratic primary,
the Pulaski County Klan, insisting on unified support by members for one
candidate, secured the Democratic nomination for every one of its candidates. This ensured KKK control over county government, the county delegation in the general assembly, and the congressional district. Across the
state local Klans became involved in politics to a greater degree, making an
impact in elections from the legislature to local school boards.

As the Klan reached its political zenith, the state's politicians carefully
maneuvered to secure Klan support, but often without openly identifying
with them. In 1922 the KKK endorsed the incumbent governor, Thomas C.
McRae. McRae did not actively seek the endorsement, although his private
secretary was a Klan member. His program, however, was pitched to secure
their support. McRae's platform in 1922 emphasized strict law enforcement,
including prohibition laws, and government economy. This was enough for
the Klan to consider him a friend, even though not himself a member of

the organization. McRae may well have won without Klan support, but with it he crushed his opponent in the Democratic primary.

Until 1924 the Klan was able to operate politically through the Democratic Party, but that year they actually moved to take over the party by holding an internal vote to determine which candidates should receive Klan support in the primary. By unifying all members for a single candidate, the organization could have secured enormous power within the party. However, the 1924 election proved to be a turning point for the KKK's political influence. Potential candidates for the Democratic nomination who did not secure Klan backing moved to organize a slate that was avowedly anti-Klan. In the campaign James G. Ferguson, a Klansman himself, blasted the organization's leadership, its efforts at controlling state politics, and its use of what he considered to be a corrupt electoral system for determining their preferred candidates. Other Democratic Klansmen were reluctant to give the leadership so much power, thus splitting their vote, and Secretary of State Tom J. Terral emerged from a large number of candidates as the Democratic Party's nominee rather than the KKK's candidate.

Defeat in 1924 helped break up Klan power. The Democratic Party, however, also moved to ensure that no rival emerged for its control of the state government. Democrats had effectively dealt with dissent in the past, and once again, as public sentiment moved in a direction that prompted protest, the leadership maneuvered to cut off any gains dissenters might make. Democratic candidates in the 1920s did not back away completely from the Progressive revolution in government, but they sounded increasingly conservative on social issues. Fiscal and social conservatism with a continued use of government to solve the state's problems became the core of Democratic politics. Restrained fiscal policies, though, provided a major barrier to carrying out changes that might have quickly and efficiently dealt with the issues of critical concern.

Thomas C. McRae set the tone for state government throughout the 1920s in his inaugural address in January 1921. In his comments on law enforcement, Governor McRae clearly indicated conservative fears and suspicions: "We want progressivism in Arkansas" and "the benefits that modern education and invention have given," he said. "But we should not allow this desire for things modern to destroy or remove any of the character building teachings and customs that were good and valuable in years that are gone, and will be good and valuable in the years to come." McRae did not specify exactly what all these teachings and customs were, but he did state clearly his desire to punish criminals. "Those who uphold the law," he said, "must have justice also, and justice to them includes protection of them through the proper punishment of criminals." He went on to lecture Arkansans on the limits of laws, however, encouraging them to teach their children respect for authority, religion and sacred things, and the "sturdy home discipline of our forefathers."

On the other hand, McRae concluded that there were areas in which the government still had to play a role in solving the state's problems. Education, which was needed to end illiteracy, to provide vocational training, and to improve physical conditioning of students, was "our greatest abstract problem." Highway construction was a close second.

McRae recognized that the key challenge facing government at this time was finance. When he took office, he found that requests for appropriated funds already were $500,000 in excess of the actual revenue of the state. However, in a period of economic crisis, raising additional monies was difficult. McRae's recommendations to the legislature set the conservative fiscal tone for his administration and provided a model for his successors: Essentially, money had to be saved. Government had to be made more efficient. Boards and commissions that were unnecessary had to be eliminated. Some functions of state government must be turned over to the federal government. Neither McRae nor his successors considered a general increase in taxes, although they did examine the possibilities of restructuring the state assessment system and looked at a wide variety of special fees that might increase government income.

Within the much narrower framework imposed by the conservative governors of the 1920s, the state continued to move forward. Improvements did take place. As recognized by Governor McRae, the state could not back away from its efforts to maintain schools and build roads. The problem, however, was how to finance these projects.

The most pressing issue, in terms of both priority and financing, was education. By the 1920s support for schools represented the single biggest cost for state government. In the 1919–1920 biennium, appropriations for the state's common schools and universities constituted over 31 percent of the budget. As the tax base was cut, legislators struggled to find the money necessary to keep schools even at the level they had reached by 1920.

In 1921 Governor McRae was able to secure, despite opposition from major timber and mining companies, a severance tax on natural resources extracted from the land with the revenue allocated completely to the school fund. But this did not provide enough money, and in 1924 Governor McRae called a special session of the legislature to deal with school funding. Pushing for an income tax, McRae got instead the "Parnell Cigarette Tax," a "sin" tax on cigarettes and cigars, and even that required another special session after the first law was declared unconstitutional. Gov. Thomas Terrell continued the search for educational funds, asking for taxes on chewing gum and cosmetics. It was not until Gov. Harvey Parnell managed to obtain an income tax in 1929 that significant new revenue was secured. However, that would turn out to be too late to produce any major changes in the schools.

A decade of work with limited resources produced some improvements. More money was spent on education, but many of the problems remained. By the 1930s educators could look at the state's schools and find there were still too many districts dividing up too little money. The inadequacy of rural to urban schools was still present, both in terms of funding and the resulting performance of students. The disparity in funding for black schools was even more pronounced. In 1931 I. T. Gilliam, the education research secretary for the black Arkansas State Teachers Association, reported the continuing underfunding of rural and black schools. In that year Pulaski County, the principal urban county of the state, spent $61.41 per white student in 1930, but only $32.03 for blacks. In the rural areas the difference was even greater. In Chicot County, schools spent $54.11 for each white child and only $6.36 for each black. In effect, to be from the country or to be black and from the country offered a very limited chance for an adequate education.

Another pressing demand was the development of good highways to accommodate the rapidly expanding automobile and truck traffic already beginning to erode the position of railroads as the primary source of transportation in the nation. Politicians at the local and state level were well aware of the importance of transportation in producing a favorable economic environment, and business interests everywhere encouraged the government to help finance an improved road system. While the State Highway Commission had been created in 1913 and an actual system begun, it was not until a special session in October 1923 that the general assembly responded to the challenge. At the request of Gov. Thomas McRae, who was seeking to take advantage of federal funding for road construction, the legislature passed the Harrelson Highway Act, placing the entire state into a unified highway system and creating a state highway fund financed by automobile registration fees and taxes on gasoline and oil.

The Harrelson Act was supplemented in 1927 with legislation proposed by Governor Martineau that strengthened the highway commission, allowed it to issue bonds for the construction of highways, and also assumed the existing debts of the local improvement districts that had been responsible for road construction prior to 1923. The Harrelson and Martineau legislation once again reflected the fiscal constraints on all government activities.

Finance was always at the heart of governmental problems through the 1920s. State government could be cut back only so much, finding revenues to support what remained was a continuing problem. Governor after governor tinkered with the system and eventually urged revisions of tax laws. McRae went so far as to argue that property taxes no longer reflected the true basis of wealth in a modern community. Tangible property meant little compared with the other forms of wealth that were part of the modern economy. McRae urged new taxes—insurance, inheritance, income, business and franchise—if the state was going to pay for its services. The legislature proved resistant to any significant alterations, however. As they had done with the schools and the highways, taxes on users or taxes on "sin" usually could secure support. General increases in tax rates or any major change in the system of assessments died quickly at Little Rock. As a result, while government agencies continued to struggle with the state's myriad problems, they did so with inadequate financial support. Progressivism had not really died, but it had to exist within the framework of serious fiscal constraint.

Events through the 1920s had brought the major trends established in the New South era to a virtual halt. Then, economic growth and the many government efforts that depended on tax revenues received a fatal blow with the beginning of the Great Depression, marked by the New York Stock Market collapse of October 1929. Since the state's economy had already experienced serious problems through the 1920s, Arkansans really did not even notice the fall in stock prices. The press hardly covered it. For Arkansans it simply looked like the rest of the nation was joining them in economic hard times. While the crash itself did not seem to affect the lives of Arkansans, its implications were felt immediately: an already bad economy quickly fell to lower levels.

The effects of the national depression were almost immediate. Consumer demand spiraled downward, pushing down the prices of agricultural commodities. Cotton, which had sagged throughout the 1920s and was at nineteen cents in 1929, dropped to thirteen cents in 1930, eight-and-one-half cents in 1931, and was down to six cents by 1932. The prices for other crops followed this same path. Demand for the state's industrial products fell too, with the result that many companies laid off workers. By 1933 a quarter of a million Arkansans were out of work and looking for jobs through the federal government.

To make matters worse, banking failures made it difficult for farmers to secure additional credit. In the past a bad year simply meant the farmer went back to the bank and refinanced, ready to try again. Now, loans on crops and farm mortgages were difficult to acquire. Financial institutions that made agricultural loans in Arkansas, already weakened by the state's general economic situation, were further strained, and many failed. The worst banking failures were those of Caldwell and Company, a holding company that controlled Memphis banks which had loaned heavily to Delta farmers, and American Exchange Bank of Little Rock, which had acquired controlling interest in about forty-three Arkansas institutions that were heavily involved in farm loans. Both of these took their associated banks down with them. Between 1929 and 1933, 42 percent of the state's private banks closed their doors.

If all this were not enough, in 1930 the state's farmers were again plagued by bad weather. In May, record rains ruined crops on low lands and water-logged high ground. These rains were followed by a drought, with no additional precipitation falling in much of the state until the following November. The results for at least one farmer was a half crop of cotton, no corn, and no hay. A contemporary noted that tenants were hit hardest and many of them wound up fishing in order to obtain food for themselves and their families.

Conditions among affected farmers were severe and many persons were pushed virtually to the edge of starvation. What became known as the "England Riot" exemplified the desperation of many. In January 1930 three hundred farmers from Lonoke County came to the town of England seeking aid from the Red Cross. Finding that unavailable, they demanded that merchants give them food to feed their families. The merchants, perhaps fearing violence, distributed food and received reimbursements from the Red Cross. This solution, however, did not solve the statewide problem.

By February 1931 the Red Cross in Arkansas reported that it had provided food allowances for some 519,000 persons statewide. The plight of small farmers and sharecroppers in the plantation region was particularly difficult. In St. Francis County half of the farm population was receiving relief from the Red Cross. The crisis caused by the drought of 1930 proved short lived, and by April of 1931 the press and politicians indicated that they believed the immediate threat of starvation among many persons had been diminished. The general agricultural problem, however, remained and continued to intensify.

One of the factors adding to the farm problem was that many individuals who found themselves out of work in the industrial communities outside the state appear to have returned home as the depression deepened. As a result, the farm population increased between 1930 and 1931. While times were hard on the farm, there was at least the possibility that people could provide themselves with enough food to survive.

The people of the towns were not in much better shape. Rural markets dried up. Town merchants had no better luck securing credit than their rural neighbors. Manufacturers were caught in the same bind. Given such circumstances, even that section of the population, which had always been most optimistic and most ready for change, found it hard to maintain any great hopes for the future.

Quickly proving itself a catastrophe of massive proportions, the Depression produced a revolution in Arkansas's economy and society. The crisis dislocated the state's rural population and broke up the order that had made change so difficult, literally destroying aspects of the old society. It forced upon the state a wide variety of social and political innovations. When combined with the introduction of new technologies and continuing changes that resulted from World War II, the years after 1929 and through the 1960s saw the final demise of the old order and the emergence of a new Arkansas—not necessarily the one envisioned by the advocates of the New South back in the 1880s, but new nonetheless.

The onset of the Depression ended an era in Arkansas history. Despite the state's detractors, Arkansans made remarkable strides between 1874 and 1929 in their efforts to create greater prosperity and to improve their lives. Their approaches to these goals were almost exactly the same as people throughout the United States. They tried to diversify their economy. They sought closer links with the national economy and its culture. Ultimately, they were willing to use government to address some of the persistent problems they faced.

Arkansas never achieved the success that the proponents for change wanted. It was not for want of will or even ingenuity, however. The model of development they used was almost the same as that used by more successful states. In the end, the extent of change that was necessary was too great, Arkansans had to come from too far back. At the end of Reconstruction almost the whole of Arkansas's economy was based on agriculture. The society associated with that economy provided few supports for innovation. The extent of economic development necessary to displace agriculture was enormous, the reorganization of society essential to provide support for such a development was massive. In both areas, despite the limits imposed by the strength of the agrarian-rural world, alterations occurred. The economic diversification and the consequent institutional adjustments of society may have appeared minimal compared to the persisting agrarian and rural world that dominated the state. Still, Arkansans had begun to move in a new direction, toward a closer connection to the trends dominating the national economy and society. That course might have seemed terribly slow at times, but the course that had been set, despite setbacks, was unalterable.

Subsequent years would see the continuation of the movement begun with such hope in the 1870s. Given its limits, the New South effort in Arkansas actually was remarkably successful.

Bibliographic Essay

A considerable amount of material has been published on the history of Arkansas during the period considered by this study, but the topical treatment is uneasy and weighted toward political works. There is no study of the era that has attempted to synthesize the existing literature or to provide an analytical framework within which the years from 1874 to 1929 may be understood. The following bibliography contains articles and books that have been directly influential in the writing of this volume and that should be examined by the student seeking to further explore particular issues. For a more comprehensive bibliographic treatment, the reader should consult Michael B. Dougan, Tom W. Dillard, and Timothy G. Nutt, *Arkansas History: An Annotated Bibliography* (Westport, Conn.: Greenwood Press, 1995).

Introduction

There have been numerous essays that have sought to characterize and explain the major trends in late-nineteenth- and early-twentieth-century Arkansas history, although no specific studies of this era. For such works see E. E. Dale, "Arkansas: The Myth and the State," *Arkansas Historical Quarterly* 12 (Spring 1953): 8–29; Lee A. Dew, "On a Slow Train Through Arkansas," *AHQ* 39 (Summer 1980): 125–35; E. J. Friedlander, "The Miasmatic Jungles, Reactions to H. L. Mencken's 1921 Attack," *AHQ* 38 (Spring 1979): 63–71; Bob Lancaster, "Bare Feet and Slow Trains," *Arkansas Times* 13 (June 1987): 34–41; William Foy Lisenby, "A Survey of Arkansas's Image Problem," *AHQ* 30 (Spring 1971): 60–71. For similar reactions in an earlier period see C. Fred Williams, "The Bear State Image: Arkansas in the Nineteenth Century," *AHQ* 39 (Summer 1980): 99–111. Michael Dougan, *Arkansas Odyssey* (Little Rock: Rose Press, 1995), although a general history of the state, is the only book-length examination of Arkansas that provides an analysis and historical assessment of this period.

Arkansas Faces a New Era

There are amazingly few scholarly studies of rural life and institutions in Arkansas. Janet Allured, "Ozark Women and the Companionate Family in the Arkansas Hills, 1870–1910," *AHQ* 47 (Autumn 1988): 230–56, looks at changing family life during these years. Dealing with both rural and urban communities, Fon L. Gordon, *Caste & Class: The Black Experience in Arkansas, 1880–1920* (Athens: University of Georgia Press, 1995), provides the best analysis of the dynamics of life among African-Americans.

There are, however, numerous reminiscences, memoirs, and a few published collections of letters that cover this era. Octave Thanet, "Plantation Life in Arkansas," *Atlantic Monthly* 60 (July 1891): 32–49, is an interesting contemporary essay on rural life in eastern Arkansas. Among useful memoirs are Dan Dennington, *Over Lightly, One More Time: Recollections of a Southwestern Tenant Farmer's Son, 1915–1934,* Rebecca D. Landes, ed. (Republic, Mo.: Rebecca D. Landes, 1990); J. J. Propps, "My Childhood and Youth in Arkansas," *AHQ* 26 (Winter 1967): 310–52, a story of life in Howard County; and Pearl Etheridge Young, "Memories of an Ashley County Childhood," *AHQ* 16 (Winter 1957): 342–57 and 18 (Winter 1959): 375–400, providing information on both rural and town life. Two of the most important collections of letters dealing with rural life, although from the perspective of educated merchant families, may be found in Sarah M. Fountain, ed., *Sisters, Seeds, & Cedars: Rediscovering Nineteenth-Century Life through Correspondence from Rural Arkansas and Alabama* (Conway: University of Central Arkansas Press, 1995), detailing the lives of members of the Boddie family in Ouachita County, and Elizabeth Paisley Huckaby and Ethel C. Simpson, ed., *Tulip Evermore: Emma Butler and William Paisley, Their Lives in Letters, 1857–1887* (Fayetteville: University of Arkansas Press, 1985), dealing with the Butler and Paisley families, merchants and sometime-farmers who lived in Dallas County and elsewhere in southwestern Arkansas.

Few materials deal directly with the lives of African-American farm life. Those that exist document primarily the lives of the more successful. For the life of one such individual see Ulysses S. Bond, "Highlights in the Life of Scott Bond," *AHQ* 21 (Summer 1962): 144–52, and for a fuller treatment, Dan A. Rudd and Theo Bond, *From Slavery to Wealth: the Life of Scott Bond* (Madison, Ark.: n.p., 1917). For the struggles of one black tenant-farming family see William Pickens, *Bursting Bonds* (Boston: Jordan and More Press, 1923). See also Phil James, "Pickens Black, Planter," *Stream of History* 16 (October 1978): 11–19. Ruth Polk Patterson, *The Seed of Sally Good'n: A Black Family of Arkansas, 1833–1953* (Lexington: The University Press of Kentucky, 1985), is the history of a land-owning African-American family.

As in the case of rural society, there is little scholarly work on the state's farm economy in this era. Although it focuses on a later period, Benson Y. Landis and George Edmund Haynes, *Cotton-Growing Communities* (New York: The Federal Council of Churches of Christ in America, 1935), offer a studied insight into farm economics and labor relationships that were probably typical of the nineteenth as well as the twentieth century.

The forces that were responsible for the constitution of 1874 and the implications of the document that they prepared are well-examined in Walter Nunn, "The Constitutional Convention of 1874," *AHQ* 17 (1968): 177–204. Other aspects of Bourbon control and contemporary political issues may be found in Garland E. Bayliss, "Post Reconstruction Repudiation: Evil Blot or Financial Necessity?" *AHQ* 23 (Autumn 1964): 243–59, and "The Arkansas State Penitentiary Under Democratic Control," *AHQ* 24 (Autumn 1975): 195–213; Jane Zimmerman, "The Convict Lease System in Arkansas and the Fight for Abolition," *AHQ* 8 (Autumn 1949): 171–88; and Felton D. Freeman, "Immigration to Arkansas," *AHQ* 8 (Autumn 1949): 210–19.

Forces of Change

Studies of economic changes between 1875 and 1929 are as rare as those of agriculture. Although limited, Charles Hillman Brough, "The Industrial History of Arkansas," *Publications of the Arkansas Historical Association* 1 (1906): 191–229, provides an overview of what was taking place by a contemporary political and educational leader.

There are, however, numerous studies that deal with particular aspects of the economic transition. Arkansas railroads are examined by Stephen E. Wood, particularly "The Development of Arkansas Railroads," *AHQ* 7 (Summer 1948): 103–40, and 7 (Autumn 1948): 155–93. Lee A. Dew, "From Trails to Rails in Eureka Springs," *AHQ* 41 (Autumn 1982): 203–15; and Ellen Compton Shipley, "The Pleasures of Prosperity, Bella Vista, Arkansas, 1917–1929," *AHQ* 37 (Summer 1978): 99–129, show aspects of the developing spa and resort industry. Insights to the Arkansas coal industry may be found in Bob Besom, "Little Rock Businessmen Invest in Coal: Harmon L. Remmel and the Arkansas Anthracite Coal Company, 1905–1923," *AHQ* 47 (Autumn 1988): 273–87.

The one area of economic development that has attracted the most attention is the timber industry. The best overview is Kenneth L. Smith, *Sawmill: The Story of Cutting the Last Great Virgin Forest East of the Rockies* (Fayetteville: University of Arkansas Press, 1986), even though it deals primarily with efforts in the Ouachita Mountains. See also Corliss C. Curry, "Early Timber Operations in Southeast Arkansas," *AHQ* 19 (Summer 1960): 111–18; and George Walter Balogh, "Crossett: The Community, the Company, and Change," *AHQ* 44 (Summer 1985): 156–74. Walter L. Brown, "Life of an Arkansas Logger in 1901," *AHQ* 21 (Spring 1962): 44–74, provides insight into the industry from the perspective of a logger.

Practically nothing has been written about the beginnings of manufacturing or the explosion of urban economies. James W. Leslie, "Cotton Compresses of Pine Bluff," *Jefferson County Historical Quarterly* 8 (1980): 9–14, is a notable exception. For a study of some of the characteristics of the men engaged in industrial efforts, see Carl H. Moneyhon, "The Creators of the New South in Arkansas: Industrial Boosterism, 1875–1885," *AHQ* 55 (Winter 1996), 383–409.

Urban Development

There is no study of urbanization in Arkansas, but to understand this phenomenon the student must begin with John W. Graves, *Town and Country; Race Relations and Urban Development in Arkansas 1865–1900* (Fayetteville: University of Arkansas Press, 1990). Although Graves is primarily interested in differences in race relations between rural and urban areas, his work offers an excellent overview of urban development and conditions in the late nineteenth century. Among the few studies of urban processes that exist, see Cheryl Griffith Nichols, "Pulaski Heights: Early Suburban Development in Little Rock, Arkansas," *AHQ* 41 (Summer 1982): 129–45; and E. F. (Ed) Chesnutt, "Little Rock Gets Electric Lights," *AHQ* 42 (Autumn 1983): 237–53.

There are a few studies that touch upon urban society. Carolyn Gray LeMaster, *A Corner of the Tapestry: A History of the Jewish Experience in Arkansas, 1820s–1990s* (Fayetteville: University of Arkansas Press, 1994), provides a useful history of the state's Jewish community, primarily an urban group. Some information on urban women is provided in Clara B. Eno, "Some Accomplishments of Arkansas Federation of Women's Clubs," *AHQ* 2 (September 1943): 255–57; see also Mrs. Frederick Hanger, *A History of the Arkansas Federation of Women's Clubs*. Marilyn Martin, "From Altruism to Activism: The Contributions of Literary Clubs to Arkansas Public Libraries, 1885–1935," *AHQ* 55 (Spring 1996): 64–94, points up the increase in activities that took place among urban women.

For some insights into the world of the black middle class, in addition to the previously cited study by Fon Gordon, see Willard B. Gatewood Jr., "Arkansas Negroes in the 1890s: Documents," *AHQ* 33 (Winter 1974): 292–325, and "Frederick Douglass in Arkansas," *AHQ* 41 (Winter 1992): 303–15. There are several studies of major African-American community leaders—see Tom W. Dillard, *"Golden Prospects and Fraternal Amenities:* Mifflin W. Gibbs's Arkansas Years," *AHQ* 35 (Winter 1976): 307–33, and "Scipio A. Jones," *AHQ* 31 (Autumn 1972): 201–19; and C. Calvin Smith, "John E. Bush: the Politician and the Man, 1880–1916," *AHQ* 54 (Summer 1995): 115–33. An interesting insight into black culture within the urban framework may be found in Judith Anne Still, "Carrie Still Shepperson: The Hollows of Her Footsteps," *AHQ* 42 (Spring 1983): 37–46.

Physicians are the only professional group that have been studied. David M. Moyers, "From Quackery to Qualification: Arkansas Medical and Drug Legislation, 1881–1909," *AHQ* 35 (Spring 1976): 3–26, provides information on their efforts.

Deteriorating race relations have received considerable attention. The struggle to determine the nature of African-American education may be found in Thomas Rothrock, "Joseph Carter Corbin and Negro Education in the University of Arkansas," *AHQ* 30 (Winter 1971): 277–314; and Elizabeth L. Wheeler, "Isaac Fisher: The Frustrations of a Negro Educator at Branch Normal College, 1902–1911," *AHQ* 51 (Spring 1982): 3–50. Disfranchisement and segregation are shown in John W. Graves, "Negro Disfranchisement in Arkansas," *AHQ* 26 (Autumn 1967): 199–25, and "The Arkansas Separate Coach Law of 1891," *AHQ* 32 (Summer 1973): 148–65; see also Tom Dillard, "To the Back of the Elephant: Racial Conflict in the Arkansas Republican Party," *AHQ* 33 (Spring 1974): 3–15.

While there is little scholarly analysis of town life in Arkansas there have been many descriptions of these communities. Among the best personal memoirs are Sam Boucher, "Memories of Pine Bluff, Arkansas 1913 to 1916," *Jefferson County Historical Quarterly* 13 (1985): 12–23; Boyce House, "A Small Arkansas Town [Brinkley] 50 Years Ago," *AHQ* 18 (Autumn 1959): 291–307, "In a Little Town Long Ago," *AHQ* 19 (Summer 1960): 151–68, and "Arkansas Boyhood, Long Ago," *AHQ* 20 (Summer 1961): 172–81; Arthur Murray, "City of Pine Bluff: Descriptive," *Jefferson County Historical Quarterly* 13 (1985), 4–15; Donald Murray, "Recalling My Days in Jonesboro," *Craighead County Historical Quarterly* 9 (Summer 1971): 7–17; Neill Phillips, "What It Was Like: Newport, Arkansas— Not So Long Ago," *Stream of History* 10 (July 1972): 35–40; 10 (October 1972): 29–39; 11 (October 1973): 29–38; 11 (May 1973): 31–39; 11 (July 1973): 35–40; 10 (October 1973): 37–39; 12 (January 1974: 33–39; and 12 (April 1974): 17–21; Mrs. Hay W. Smith, "Life in Little Rock in the Gay Nineties," *Pulaski County Historical Review* 5 (December 1957): 69–74; and Faye Wallis, "I Remember Pine Bluff," *Jefferson County Historical Quarterly* 11 (1983): 11–17. Some insights into a small mountain community are provided in Ethel Frances Jones, "The Elixir of Youth," *AHQ* 23 (Autumn 1964): 212–42. Although it is not as rich in details as her look at Arkansas rural life, Octave Thanet, "Town Life in Arkansas," *Atlantic Monthly* 68 (September 1891): 332–40, offers some overview of a smaller town.

Plight of the Farmers

Little has been written about actual agricultural conditions in Arkansas in the late nine-teenth century. Any study must consult the vast statistical and qualitative analysis presented by the Bureau of the Census and the Department of Agriculture. Among all of these, Eugene W. Hilgard, *Report on Cotton Production in the United States* (Washington: Government Printing Office, 1884), is particularly invaluable.

Development of the Grand Prairie may be found in Ernest E. Sampson, "Half a Century on Grand Prairie," *AHQ* 14 (Spring 1955): 32–37.

An excellent example of historical archaeology that offers insights into farm life through material culture is Leslie C. Stewart-Abernathy, *The Moser Farmstead, Independent but Not Isolated: The Archeology of a Late Nineteenth Century Ozark Farmstead. Arkansas Archeological Survey Research, Series No. 26* (Fayetteville: Arkansas Archeological Survey, 1986). Jerome C. Rose, ed., *Gone to a Better Land: A Biohistory of a Rural Black Cemetery in the Post-Reconstruction South. Arkansas Archeological Survey Research Series, No. 25.* (Fayetteville: Arkansas Archeological Survey, 1985), uses forensic archaeology to provide its own superb assessment of rural life.

The annual reports of the Arkansas superintendent of education furnish essential information on the problems of education in the state. The Department of the Interior, Bureau of Education's study, *The Public School System of Arkansas*, 2 vols. (Washington, D.C.: Government Printing Office, 1923), is also a critical document on schools. For the personal experiences of a rural teacher see Roy V. Simpson, "Reminiscences of a Hill Country School Teacher," *AHQ* 27 (Summer 1968): 146–74. There are few scholarly treatments of the early school system, however. One exception is John W. Payne, "Poor-Man's Pedagogy: Teachers' Institutes in Arkansas," *AHQ* 14 (Autumn 1955); 195–206, an examination of early efforts at improving teacher training.

Working Class Protest in the New Arkansas

Of all aspects of Arkansas history, the greatest amount of attention by historians has been on the agricultural reform movement. For roots of protest see Judith Barjenbruch, "The Greenback Political Movement: An Arkansas View," *AHQ* 26 (Summer 1977): 107–22. A brief history of the Patrons of Husbandry in Arkansas is Granville D. Davis, "The Granger Movement in Arkansas," *AHQ* 4 (Winter 1945): 340–52. Berton E. Henningson Jr., "Northwest Arkansas and the Brothers of Freedom: The Roots of a Farmer Movement," *AHQ* 34 (Winter 1975): 304–24, and "'Root Hog or Die': The Brothers of Freedom and the 1884 Arkansas Election," *AHQ* 45 (Autumn 1986): 197–216, provides a look at the Brothers of Freedom and its foray into politics in 1884. For efforts by African-Americans to organize and the results, see William F. Holmes, "The Arkansas Cotton Pickers Strike of 1891 and the Demise of the Colored Farmers Alliance," *AHQ* 32 (Summer 1973): 107–19.

An early overview of the Wheel is Theodore Saloutos, "The Agricultural Wheel in Arkansas," *AHQ* 2 (June 1943): 127–40. Saloutos has largely been replaced by the work of F. Clark Elkins, "Arkansas Farmers Organize for Action," *AHQ* 13 (Autumn 1954): 231–48, "The Agricultural Wheel: County Politics and Consolidation, 1884–1885," *AHQ* 29 (Spring 1970): 152–75, and "State Politics and the Agricultural Wheel," *AHQ* 38 (Autumn 1979): 248–58.

Organized labor, which became a component of the agrarian protest movement, has been addressed in a variety of articles. See especially Thomas S. Baskett Jr., *"Miners Stay Away!* W. B. W. Heartsill and the Last Years of the Arkansas Knights of Labor, 1892–1896," *AHQ* 42 (Summer 1983): 107–33. See also William W. Rogers, "Negro Knights of Labor in Arkansas: A Case Study of the 'Miscellaneous' Strike," *Labor History* 10 (Summer 1969): 489–504; and Ralph V. Turner and William W. Rogers, "Arkansas Labor in Revolt: Little Rock and the Great Southwestern Strike," *AHQ* 24 (Spring 1965): 29–46.

Clifton Paisley, "The Political Wheelers and Arkansas' Election of 1888," *AHQ* 25 (Spring 1966): 4–21, details how these various movements came together in 1888 to challenge Democratic political hegemony and chronicles the means used by the dominant party to maintain control of state government.

For a discussion of Jeff Davis's political appeal, see Richard L. Niswonger, "A Study in Southern Demaguery: Jeff Davis of Arkansas," *AHQ* 39 (Summer 1980): 114–24 and Calvin R. Ledbetter, "Jeff Davis and the Politics of Combat," *AHQ* 33 (Spring 1974): 14–37. The best modern overview of Davis is Raymond Arsenault, *The Wild Ass of the*

Ozarks: Jeff Davis and the Social Bases of Southern Politics (Philadelphia: Temple University Press, 1984).

Turn-of-the-Century Prosperity and Challenges

Although it examines a part of the state only opened to development during the late nineteenth and early twentieth century, Jeannie M. Whayne, *A New Plantation South: Land, Labor, and Federal Favor in Twentieth-Century Arkansas* (Charlottesville and London: University Press of Virginia, 1996) provides a superb overview of the problems of the cotton farmer during these years. Information on the clearing of eastern Arkansas land may be found in William M. Clements and Larry D. Ball, "'This Was the Beginning of Clearing of Land': The Development and Use of the East Arkansas Stump Saw," *AHQ* 45 (Spring 1986): 41–52. See also S. E. Simonson, "Origin of Drainage Projects in Mississippi County," *AHQ* 5 (Winter 1946): 263–73.

Rice farming has been treated in Florence L. Rosencrantz, "The Rice Industry in Arkansas," *AHQ* 5 (Summer 1946): 123–37. Fuller's own story of how he started rice farming may be found in "Early Rice Farming on Grand Prairie," *AHQ* 14 (Spring 1955): 72–74. Henry C. Dethloff, "Rice Revolution in the Southwest, 1880–1910," *AHQ* 29 (Spring 1970): 66–75, is the best scholarly look at this development.

Thomas Rothrock, "A King That Was," *AHQ* 33 (Winter 1974), 326–33 discusses orchard operations in northwestern Arkansas.

The importance of the railroads in opening new lands during these years may be seen in Lawrence R. Handley, "Settlement across Northern Arkansas as Influenced by the Missouri & North Arkansas Railroad," *AHQ* 33 (Winter 1974): 274–92, and Lee A. Dew, "The J.L.C. and E.R.R. and the Opening of the 'Sunk Lands' of Northeast Arkansas," *AHQ* 27 (Spring 1968); 22–39.

Some attention has been paid to new extractive industries. For the oil and gas industry see Gerald Forbes, "Brief History of the Petroleum Industry in Arkansas," *AHQ* 1 (Spring 1942): 28–40. The early bauxite industry is shown in Gordon Bachus, "Background and Early History of a Company Town: Bauxite, Arkansas, a Brief History of the Aluminum Industry," *AHQ* 27 (Winter 1968): 330–57.

The history of the Climber Motor Car Company, which represented a peak in industrial development and at the same time showed the weaknesses of the industrial effort, may be found in Ed. Faulker, "The Climber: A Chapter in Arkansas Automotive History," *AHQ* 29 (Autumn 1970): 215–25.

Samuel A. Sizer, "'This is Union Man's Country' Sebastian County 1914," *AHQ* 17 (Winter 1968): 306–29, shows continuing labor strife.

Studies of racial problems in the state during the twentieth century primarily focus on the Elaine Riot. The best modern study of this is Richard C. Cortner, *A Mob Intent on Death: The NAACP and the Arkansas Riot Cases* (Middletown, Conn.: Wesleyan University Press, 1988). Older studies include O. A. Rogers Jr., "The Elaine Race Riots of 1919," *AHQ* 19 (Summer 1960), 142; and J. W. and Dorothy J. Butts, "The Underlying

Causes of the Elaine Riot of 1919," *AHQ* 20 (Spring 1961), 95–104. A particularly interesting primary source on this crisis is Walter F. White, "'Massacring Whites' in Arkansas," *Nation* 109 (December 6, 1919), 715. Military reports may be found in Ralph H. Desmaris, ed., "Military Intelligence Reports on Arkansas Riots: 1919–1920," *AHQ* 33 (Summer 1974): 175–91.

Little has been written about Arkansas in World War I. The activities of the Council of Defense are detailed in Gerald Senn, "Molders of Thought Directors of Action: The Arkansas Council of Defense, 1917–1918," *AHQ* 36 (Autumn 1977): 280–90. A case study of mobilization is David O. Demuth, "An Arkansas County Mobilizes: Saline County, Arkansas, 1917–1918," *AHQ* 36 (Autumn 1977): 211–33. James F. Willis, "The Cleburne County Draft War," *AHQ* 26 (Spring 1967): 24–39, indicates that all Arkansans did not enter gladly into the fray.

A discussion of the type of religious change inherent in the new urban setting is shown in Larry R. Hayward, "F. E. Maddox: Chaplain of Progress, 1908," *AHQ* 38 (Summer 1979): 146–66.

The Progressive Years

Much has been written about Progressivism, although its overall history in Arkansas remains undone.

For the roots of women's participation see Janie Synatzske Evins, "Arkansas Women: Their Contribution to Society, Politics and Business, 1865–1900," *AHQ* 44 (Summer 1985): 118–33. The suffrage movement is dealt with in A. Elisabeth Taylor, "The Woman Suffrage Movement in Arkansas," *AHQ* 15 (Spring 1956): 17–52. Insight to one of the suffrage advocates may be found in Dorsey D. Jones, "Catherine Campbell Cunningham, Advocate of Equal Rights for Women," *AHQ* 12 (Summer 1953): 85–90. For less militant women Progressives, see Frances M. Ross, "The New Woman as Club Woman and Social Activist in Turn of the Century Arkansas," *AHQ* 50 (Winter 1991): 317–51.

For the socialist roots of Progressivism see G. Gregory Kiser, "The Socialist Party in Arkansas, 1900–1912," *AHQ* 40 (Summer 1981): 119–53.

Urban origins and the forces at work in towns may be seen in Martha W. Rimmer, "Progressivism Comes to Little Rock: The Election of 1911," *Pulaski County Historical Review* 25 (September 1977), 49–60, and "Progressivism in Little Rock: The War against Vice," *Pulaski County Historical Review* 25 (December 1977): 65–72.

Stuart Towns, "Joseph T. Robinson and Arkansas Politics: 1912–1913," *AHQ* 24 (Winter 1965): 291–307 and Richard L. Niswonger, "William F. Kirby, Arkansas's Maverick Senator," *AHQ* 37 (Autumn 1978): 252–63, show aspects of politics in the early twentieth century. There are several excellent recent biographies of the state's Progressive governors. These include Calvin R. Ledbetter, *Carpenter from Conway: George Washington Donaghey as Governor of Arkansas, 1909–1913* (Fayetteville: University of Arkansas

Press, 1993), and William Foy Lisenby, *Charles Hillman Brough: A Biography* (Fayetteville: University of Arkansas Press, 1996). Brough, in fact, has probably received more attention than any other single Arkansas politician for this period. See Charles O. Cook, "'The Glory of the Old South and the Greatness of the New': Reform and the Divided Mind of Charles Hillman Brough," *AHQ* 34 (Winter 1975): 225–41, and *"Boosterism and Babbittry:* Charles Hillman Brough and the 'Selling' of Arkansas," *AHQ* 37 (Spring 1978): 74–83; and Charles W. Crawford, "From Classroom to State Capitol: Charles H. Brough and the Campaign of 1916," *AHQ* 21 (Autumn 1962): 211–30. William Foy Lisenby provided earlier studies of the governor in "Brough, Baptists, and Bombast: The Election of 1928," *AHQ* 32 (Summer 1973): 120–31, and "Charles Hillman Brough as Historian," *AHQ* 35 (Summer 1976): 115–26.

The reports of the various state agencies created during the Progressive Era provide critical information on the histories of these agencies. These include the biennial and annual reports of the state way commission, superintendent of public education, and railroad commission.

Scholars have examined at least a few of the reform efforts of this period. See particularly Rod Farmer, "Direct Democracy in Arkansas, 1910–1918," *AHQ* 40 (Summer 1981): 99–118. Jane Zimmerman, "The Convict Lease System in Arkansas and the Fight for Abolition," *AHQ* 8 (Autumn 1949): 171–88; Thomas L. Baxley, "Prison Reforms during the Donaghey Administration," *AHQ* 22 (Spring 1963): 76–84; and Calvin R. Ledbetter, "The Long Struggle to End Convict Leasing in Arkansas," *AHQ* 52 (Spring 1993): 1–27, all deal with the prison system. See also Larry Cook, "Charles Hillman Brough and the Good Roads Movement in Arkansas," *Ozark Historical Review* 6 (Spring 1977): 26–35. Although not a scholarly study, Sarah H. Scholle, *The Pain in Prevention: A History of Public Health in Arkansas* (Little Rock: Arkansas Department of Public Health, 1990) is essential to understanding the development of that movement in the state. Svend Petersen, "Arkansas State Tuberculosis Sanatorium: The Nation's Largest," *AHQ* 5 (Winter 1946): 311–29, details public efforts at addressing this major health problem in the early twentieth century. See also Fred O. Henker, "The Evolution of Mental Health Care in Arkansas," *AHQ* 37 (Autumn 1978): 223–39; and William Foy Lisenby, "The First Meeting of the Arkansas Conference of Charities and Correction," *AHQ* 26 (Summer 1967): 155–61, and "The Arkansas Conference of Charities and Corrections, 1912–1937," *AHQ* 29 (Spring 1970), 39–47. A first-hand account of Progressive efforts at revising the state constitution is seen in Abe Collins, "Reminiscences of the Constitutional Convention of 1917-18," *AHQ* 1 (Summer 1942): 117–23.

Although it deals with the post-Progressive years, Ben F. Johnson III, "'All Thoughtful Citizens': The Arkansas School Reform Movement, 1921–1930," *AHQ* 46 (Summer 1987): 105–132 should be examined for its identification of the ideas that promoted Progressive reform, its demonstration of the persistence of these ideas into the 1920s, and its thoughtful analysis of the school reform movement in a broader social framework.

The End of an Era

One of the economic successes of the early 1920s was the oil industry. For a discussion of its development see A. R. and R. B. Buckalew, "The Discovery of Oil in South Arkansas, 1920–1924," *AHQ* 33 (Autumn 1974): 195–238, and Gerald Forbes, "Brief History of the Petroleum Industry in Arkansas," *AHQ* 1 (March 1942): 28–40. The development of the state's electrical system may be found in Harvey Couch and Winston P. Wilson, *Harvey Couch: The Master Builder* (Nashville: n.p., 1947).

The persistence of racial conflict in the period into the 1920s is treated by Todd E. Lewis, "Mob Justice in the 'American Congo': 'Judge Lynch' in Arkansas during the Decade after World War I," *AHQ* 52 (Summer 1993): 156–84.

The evolution controversy as it played out in Arkansas is developed fully by Calvin R. Ledbetter, "The Antievolution Law: Church and State in Arkansas," *AHQ* 38 (Winter 1979): 299–327. It may also be examined in R. Halliburton Jr., "The Adoption of Arkansas' Anti-Evolution Law," *AHQ* 23 (Autumn 1984): 271–83.

The emergence of the Ku Klux Klan may be seen in Charles C. Alexander, "White Robed Reformers: The Ku Klux Klan Comes to Arkansas, 1921–1922," *AHQ* 22 (Spring 1963): 14–15, "White Robes in Politics: The Ku Klux Klan in Arkansas, 1922–1924," *AHQ* 22 (Fall 1963): 195–214, and "Defeat, Decline, Disintegration: The Ku Klux Klan in Arkansas, 1924 and After," *AHQ* 22 (Winter 1963): 309–31.

The Great Depression has been examined by Donald Holley, "Arkansas and the Great Depression," *Historical Report of the Secretary of State,* vol. 3 (Little Rock: Arkansas Secretary of State, 1978). For a quick overview of the Depression in Arkansas see Gail S. Murray, "Forty Years Ago: The Great Depression Comes to Arkansas," *AHQ* 29 (Winter 1970): 291–312. Personal observations on the period may be found in John I. Smith, "Reminiscences of Farming and Business in the Depression, 1929–1933," *AHQ* 45 (Winter 1986): 321–29. For problems that added to the economic troubles see Nan E. Woodruff, "The Failure of Relief during the Arkansas Drought of 1930–31," *AHQ* 39 (Winter 1980): 301–13.

Index

Kansas City Southern Railroad, 27
Kelley, Henry E., 33
Ketchum Iron Company, 38
Kirby William F.: as Progressive legislator, 121; as attorney general, 121; gubernatorial candidate, 122
Knights of Labor: organized, 84; entry into politics, 84–85; efforts in coal mines, 110
Ku Klux Klan: in 1880s, 73; in the 1920s, 142–43

labor: labor conditions and wages in timber industry, 32; labor conditions and wages in coal industry, 33; labor conditions and wages in manufacturing, 39; changes in conditions in manufacturing, 84; wages after 1900, 102; problems 1900–1920, 109–10; problems after World War I, 133
labor organizations and unions: farmer organizations and strikes, 73; origins of union movement, 83; grievances, 83–84; typographers strike of 1876, 83; strikes against Iron Mountain Railroad in 1883, 84; Southwestern Railroad Strike of 1884, 84; United Mine Workers in coal fields, 110–11; Pullman Strike of 1894, 111; organization in oil fields, 139 Lafayette County, 71
Lake City (Craighead County), 98
Lawrence County, 12, 13
lead and zinc industry: location, 32; development after 1900, 100–101
Ledbetter, Calvin R., Jr., 92
Lee County, 73
Leachville (Mississippi County), 98
leisure activities: rural play, 11–12; city entertainments, 52–53
Leslie (Searcy County), 103
Lincoln County, 108
Linthicum, Daniel A., 56
Lion Oil and Refinery, 100
Literacy Law, 90
Little Rock (Pulaski County): manufacturing in, 35, 37, 39, 109; African-American businesses, 46; ethnic diversity, 41; problems, 54; professional police and fire departments, 55; public transportation, 55; water and sewage systems, 55; spending on schools, 74; manufacturing in, 101–2; population in, 102; changing culture, 103; Ku Klux Klan in, 142
Little Rock and Fort Smith Railroad, 26, 73
Little Rock Equal Suffrage Association, 49
Little Rock Chair Factory Company, 37
Little Rock Charity Hospital, 51
Little Rock Cooperage Company, 38
Little Rock Electric Street Railway Company, 55

Little Rock Foundry and Machine Shops, 37
Little Rock Lyceum Association, 52
Little Rock Oil Company, 29, 35
Little Rock Water Works, 55
Logan County, 33
Lonoke County: development in, 62; rice farming in, 97; Army Air Corps training base in, 104; England Riot in, 148
Loughborough, Mary W., 48
Loyal Legion, 43
lumber products industry: origins, 37–38; factories at turn of the century, 102
Lutherans, 50

McCracken, Isaac, 81
McDiarmid, Clara A., 49
McGehee (Desha County), 103
McKenzie's General Store, 40
McRae, Thomas: progressive gubernatorial administration, 122; background, 123; support of "Law and Order," 140; endorsed by Ku Klux Klan, 143; fiscal conservatism, 144–45; highway programs, 146; search for new sources of revenue, 147
machinery, 37–38
Maddox, Fenis E., 112
Madison (St. Francis County), 15
Madison County, 63
magazines: role of national magazines in local culture, 48, 49, 52
Magnolia (Columbia County), 15
Malvern (Hot Spring County): 30; women's suffrage movement in, 118; Ku Klux Klan in, 142
manufacturing: early development of, 23, 29, 34–39; government support of, 24; railroad contribution to, 36; value of products, 38; capital investment, 39; number of employees, 39; labor conditions and wages, 39; number of establishments, 39; expansion after 1900, 101–2; setback in 1920s, 137; stabilization and recovery, 138; collapse after 1929, 148
Marion County, 101
Martineau, John E.: gubernatorial views on economy, 138; highway program, 147
Memphis, Tenn., 27, 28
Memphis, Helena, and Louisiana Railroad, 98
Memphis and Little Rock Railroad, 25
men: farm work, 9–10; changing roles in urban society, 50
Mena (Polk County), 32, 41
Mencken, H. L., xi
Merrill, Henry, 36